NAHC

Wild Game Cookbook

edited by
Bill Miller, Dan Dietrich
Karyl Dodge, Deb Morem

designed by
Dean Peters

Published by the North American Hunting Club
Hopkins, Minnesota 55343

We would like to thank the following for their help:

Thayne Smith, for writing our special smoking wild game chapter, "Smokin' Up A Storm." Those who hunt with Thayne say that he's as good at cookin' wild game as he is at shootin' it.

Annette and Louis Bignami, for writing the special freezing wild game chapter, "Freeze It Right." The Bignami's are well-known for their wild game recipes.

Chilton Book Company, for supplying us with their kitchen tips from *The Book Of Household Hints*, by Cindy Crain Newman. Copyright 1980. Reprinted with permission of the publisher, Wallace-Homestead Division of Chilton Book Company, Radnor, Pennsylvania.

Foran Spice Company, for contributing recipes to this cookbook, and for providing "A Guide To Spices," from the National Restaurant Association and The American Spice Trade Association. Portions of "A Guide To Spices" reprinted with permission from Foran.

Contributing NAHC Members, who submitted cooking tips and more than 230 recipes for this NAHC cookbook.

NAHC Staff Members, for their behind the scenes work. Special thanks to Member Products Manager Mike Vail and Special Projects Coordinator Linda Kalinowski.

Cover photo by Tom Ulrich.

Address reprint requests and orders for additional books to:
NAHC Cookbook Editor
P.O. Box 3401 Hopkins, MN 55343

Library of Congress Catalog Card Number 89-62515
ISBN 0-914697-23-4
Copyright 1989, North American Hunting Club

The North American Hunting Club offers a line of hats for hunters. For information, write: NAHC, P.O. Box 3401, Hopkins, MN 55343.

Contents

Just The Right Amount Of Spice

Early last winter was the first time my family ever had pronghorn antelope on the dinner table. My wife simply roasted one of the tenderloins spiced with a smidgen of this and a pinch of that.

Preparing unfamiliar game meat for the first time, especially when it is to be judged by finicky young eaters, can be a gamble. I'm happy to report the kids loved the antelope roast! In fact it was such good table fare that my wife is even dropping hints that maybe I should venture west again this fall to bag another one.

I credit the delicious taste and texture of that meat to the care we took in the field to preserve it and to my wife's knowledge of the right spices to please our family. Through experience, all good wild game cooks gain a sixth sense of which spices are most appealing to their families and guests.

We know that each year NAHC Members across North America eagerly anticipate the publication of the annual *NAHC Wild Game Cookbook*. They can't wait to tantalize their friends with new recipes for the season's bag. This 1990 edition makes the eighth wild game cookbook by NAHC members, for NAHC members. It has become a staple in the cooking libraries of hundreds of thousands of NAHC members.

Just as a good cook is always looking for new recipes that will please the family even more, the NAHC staff is looking for spices that will please members even more. This edition of the *NAHC Wild Game Cookbook* is seasoned in a way you're sure to enjoy.

The meat—the *NAHC Wild Game Cookbook*—is still the same. It offers the same hardy reading NAHC members have come to expect. Now it is flavored with some subtle new spices to whet your appetite even more for the great meals it can help you prepare from this fall's harvest.

In addition to the all new wild game recipes developed and submitted by you and your fellow NAHC Members, this edition is heavily spiced with kitchen and household tips. The kind of pointers a game cook is likely to find useful while preparing meals at home, at the cabin or in front of a tent over an open fire. Tips came from NAHC members and the Chilton Book Company whose publication "The Book Of Household Hints" is chock full of great hints.

Thayne Smith, a highly skilled outdoorsman and a longtime friend of the NAHC has put together a superb chapter on smoking wild game. A heapin' helpin' of Thayne's spicy humor and advice will guide you through this ancient and delicious method of preparing all types of wild game.

More truly flavorful pizzazz is added in the chapter on freezing wild game by Lou Bignami. To age or not to age? To freeze in water or to freeze dry? To stew or to roast? To these chewy questions, Lou offers his sage advice.

Information from the Foran Spice Company lends robust flavor to a special chapter on Spices For Wild Game. Every cook can improve his or her dishes by enlisting a thorough knowledge of flavorful spices. Unique descriptions like those used in the world's finest restaurants provide you with spice names, flavors, uses and origins.

Good cooks never put anything but the very best on the table for their family and guests. The NAHC staff feels the same way about the annual cookbook they compile for NAHC members. Neither allows expense or inconvenience get in their way. The final product simply has to be the best or it doesn't get served.

Just take a bite of that jam-packed table of contents. It tells the tale of what a full meal this edition is. All of the seasonings included in this edition meld with the staple ingredients to make this cookbook the most savory yet.

I'm told that in China cooks are complimented by the loud belching of their guests at the conclusion of a feast. I'm not sure if that's true, but it is certain that no cook can continue to improve unless he or she is critiqued by the diners.

What do you think of the new spice in the *NAHC Wild Game Cookbook?* We hope you'll burp contentedly.

Please enjoy the book and the meals you prepare with it. And be sure to send us your favorite recipes to share with NAHC members next year!

Good Hunting,

Steven F. Burke
President

COOKBOOK ABBREVIATIONS

tsp.	=	teaspoon
T.	=	tablespoon
pt.	=	pint
oz.	=	ounce
lb.	=	pound
pkg.	=	package
sm.	=	small
med.	=	medium
lg.	=	large

MEASUREMENT CONVERSIONS

1 pinch	=	less than ⅛ tsp.
1 tbsp.	=	3 tsp.
2 tbsp.	=	1 oz.
4 tbsp.	=	¼ cup
5 tbsp. + 1 tsp.	=	⅓ cup
8 tbsp.	=	½ cup
10 tbsp.+ 2 tsp.	=	⅔ cup
12 tbsp.	=	¾ cup
16 tbsp.	=	1 cup

1 cup	=	8 oz.
1 pint	=	16 oz.
1 quart	=	32 oz.
1 gallon	=	128 oz.

1 cup	=	½ pint
2 cups	=	1 pint
4 cups	=	1 quart
2 pints	=	1 quart
4 pints	=	½ gallon
8 pints	=	1 gallon
4 quarts	=	1 gallon
8 gallons	=	1 bushel

Venison

More than 100 recipes from the kitchens and cabins of your fellow NAHC members. You'll fix great-tasting venison meals with recipes like "Brush Creek Tenderloin" (page 13), "Country Style Venison Stew" (page 32) or "Deer And Beer Chili" (page 63). Plus you'll find time saving cooking tips. Recipes for venison jerky (pages 88-92) are also included.

Venison Supreme

Serves: 4
Prep Time: 2 hours

> **6-8 sm. venison steaks**
> **salt and pepper**
> **½ cup of oil**
> **1 lb. of pork sausage**
> **2 lg. onions, chopped**
> **1 bell pepper, chopped**
> **4 stalks celery, chopped**
> **1½ tsp. garlic powder**
> **1½ cups water**
> **½ cup parsley**
> **½ cup green onion tops, chopped**
> **1 red apple, peeled and chopped**

Season venison with salt and pepper. Brown in a large skillet in hot oil. Remove venison, and add pork sausage. Brown. Then add onion, bell pepper, celery and garlic powder. Cook until onions are clear. Return venison to pot and add water. Simmer until venison is tender, about 1½ hours. Add parsley, green onion tops and apple. Cook for 10 more minutes.

Chris Yezzi
Greenbelt, Maryland

KEEP THE CRUMBS ON YOUR STEAKS—TO PREVENT BREAD CRUMBS FROM FALLING OFF STEAKS AND CHOPS IN THE FRYING PAN, BREAD THEM SEVERAL HOURS BEFORE USING AND PLACE THEM IN THE REFRIGERATOR.

Venison-Bacon Rolls

Serves: 3-4
Prep Time: 2 hours

MUSHROOMS ARE A GOOD ADDITION!

- 8 **venison steaks**
- 8 **strips of bacon**
  salt and pepper
- 1 **garlic clove, minced**
- 1 **med. onion, chopped**
  flour
- 3 **beef boullion cubes**
- 2 **cups boiling water**
- 1 **T. parsley**
- ¼ **tsp. marjoram**
- ¼ **tsp. dry mustard**

Pound steaks until thin enough to roll. Fry bacon strips until done but not crisp. Lay bacon on steaks. Sprinkle with salt, pepper, minced garlic and a few chunks of chopped onion. Roll steaks and dredge in flour. Brown in bacon grease. Remove and drain grease. Mix 3 boullion cubes with 2 cups boiling water. Stir until dissolved. Add parsley, marjoram, dry mustard and rest of onion. Pour into skillet and add the venison rolls. Simmer until tender, approximately 1½ hours. Serve with the sauce.

Gary Nelson
Rib Lake, Wisconsin

BETTER TRAIL BREAD—PACKING IN A LOAF OF BREAD LEAVES YOU WITH A PACK FULL OF CRUMBS. BAGELS ARE LESS LIKELY TO CRUMBLE AND ARE A TREAT ON THE TRAIL. YOU CAN USE TORTILLAS FOR ALL KINDS OF STUFF FROM MORNING TOAST TO EVENING TACOS. YOU CAN STUFF POCKETED PITA BREAD WITH PEANUT BUTTER OR CREAM CHEESE FOR A GREAT MEAL TO GO.

Grilled Venison

Serves: 4-6
Prep Time: 30 minutes

> 1 **lb. venison, cut into thin slices**
> ⅓ **cup cooking sake (rice wine)**
> ⅓ **cup vinegar**
> ⅓ **cup soy sauce**
> **red pepper**
> **other spices (optional)**
> **teriyaki sauce**

USE MORE VINEGAR IF VENISON HAS A STRONG, "GAMEY" TASTE!

Marinate venison about 20 minutes in a marinade of sake, vinegar, soy sauce and spices.

Grill the slices of venison over a charcoal grill. A grill made of chicken wire mesh is fine in that the slices of meat will not fall down between the rods. Dip the cooked meat in teriyaki sauce if you prefer. Serve with rice.

Norman Lund
Kofu Shi, Japan

Mustard Fried Venison

Serves: 4-6
Prep Time: 30 minutes

> 4-6 **venison loin steaks or chops**
> **seasoned salt**
> **pepper**
> 2 **T. Dijon style mustard**
> 1 **tsp. horseradish**
> ¼ **cup olive oil**

Wash steaks, pat dry. Season with salt and pepper. Combine mustard and horseradish. Spread this mixture on each side of steaks, to cover. Fry in hot olive oil. Poke with fork and as soon as juices run clear, the steaks are done.

Rex Morgan
Kansas City, Missouri

Deer Logs

Serves: 4
Prep Time: 1½ hours

> **4 venison steaks**
> **1 cup ricotta cheese**
> **1 cup of mozzarella cheese**
> **¼ cup cream cheese**
> **1½ tsp. garlic**
> **1 tsp. Italian seasoning**
> **½ tsp. basil**
> **1 cup onion, diced**
> **1 tsp. lemon juice**

Combine all ingredients except steaks. Spread mixture on steaks and roll up like a log. Insert toothpick to hold together. Place in covered greased pan. Bake at 300 degrees for 45 minutes. Serve.

John Davies
Hanover, Maryland

Venison Steaks In Wine

Serves: 2
Prep Time: 15-20 minutes

> **2 sm. venison steaks**
> **1 T. butter**
> **dash of fennel**
> **garlic salt**
> **basil**
> **white cooking wine**

Melt butter in frying pan over medium heat. Put steaks in pan and add fennel, garlic salt and basil. Cook for 5 to 10 minutes and add white cooking wine. Cook for 5 to 10 more minutes or until done to your liking.

Jay Crawford
Weare, New Hampshire

Venison Shanks

Serves: 4
Prep Time: 2½ hours

> **4 venison shanks**
> **salt and pepper**
> **1 cup water combined with ¾ cup Marsala or Madiera wine**
> **½ lb. fresh mushrooms, sliced**
> **¼ cup green onions, sliced**
> **¼ cup fresh parsley, chopped**
> **1 garlic clove, minced**
> **¼ tsp. rosemary**

Season shanks with salt and pepper and place on a greased baking pan. Bake uncovered at 325 degrees for one hour or until browned, turning once. Pour off all fat, if any. Pour half the wine and water mixture over the shanks, cover and bake for one hour or more. Sprinkle the shanks with the mushrooms, green onions and parsley. Combine the remaining wine and water with the garlic and rosemary and pour over the shanks, again cover and bake at 400 degrees for 30 minutes. Serve and spoon the sauce mixture over them.

Gene Leone
Walnut Creek, California

GET THE "WILD" OUT—MY HUNTING BUDDY, RON DETILLO OF KENAI, ALASKA, TOLD ME THAT TO TENDERIZE AND REMOVE THE "WILD" TASTE IN MOOSE, DEER, ANTELOPE OR ANY WILD MEAT, MARINATE THE MEAT IN ITALIAN DRESSING FOR 4 TO 6 HOURS. THEN COOK AS USUAL. WORKS BEST WITH BARBECUED MEAT.

Brush Creek Tenderloin

Serves: 2-4
Prep Time: 30 minutes

1 lb. venison tenderloin steaks, butterfly cut
dash of meat tenderizer
favorite breading mixture
2 slices of bacon
½ onion, diced
½ green pepper, diced
2 tsp. Worcestershire sauce
1 16 oz. can whole stewed tomatoes
1 can red kidney beans (optional)
salt, pepper and garlic powder

EXCELLENT OVER NOODLES OR RICE!

Beat steaks with mallet and sprinkle with meat tenderizer.
Bread tenderized steaks with favorite mixture of breading. Fry
2 slices of bacon in skillet until they are crisp and crumble. Fry
butterfly steaks for 15 to 20 minutes until done. Add diced
onions, green pepper and Worcestershire sauce after meat has
browned. Add stewed tomatoes to skillet along with kidney
beans if desired. Add small amount of garlic powder and salt
and pepper. Cook for 10 to 15 minutes with lid on. Stir as
needed to prevent burning. Serve.

Russell Choate
Glade Valley, North Carolina

VACUUM YOUR EARS—WHEN CLEANING SWEET CORN FOR
FREEZING, USE THE VACUUM CLEANER AND SMALL ROUND BRUSH
ATTACHMENT TO REMOVE HAIR FROM EACH EAR. IT'S A REAL TIMESAVER.
EACH EAR COMES OUT CLEANER, TOO.

Baked Venison Steak

Serves: 4-6
Prep Time: 2-2½ hours

> **2-3 lbs. boneless venison steaks**
> **garlic salt**
> **celery salt**
> **pepper**
> **flour**
> **¼ cup oil**
> **1 med. onion, chopped**
> **1 cup celery, thinly sliced**
> **1 cup mushrooms, sliced**
> **2 cans cream of mushroom soup**
> **1 can cheddar cheese soup**
> **2 cans water**

Cut steaks ½- to ¾-inch thick, cut in small sizes. Sprinkle the meat lightly with garlic salt, celery salt and pepper. Flour meat and brown on both sides in ¼ cup oil. When meat is brown, place in a baking dish or pan large enough to hold all items. Spread meat evenly over bottom of pan. Spread onion, celery and mushrooms over meat. In a separate dish or bowl, add cream of mushroom soup, cheese soup and water. Mix well and pour over meat and vegetables. Bake at 350 degrees for 1½ to 2 hours or until the meat is tender. Serve with your favorite vegetable and salad.

Bobby Wright
Highland, Indiana

PRESSURE COOKER PRESERVES FOOD—FOOD THAT HAS BEEN PREPARED IN A PRESSURE COOKER DOES NOT HAVE TO BE TRANSFERRED TO THE REFRIGERATOR OR ICE BOX FOR STORAGE. SIMPLY COVER THE PRESSURE COOKER AND BRING THE FOOD TO 15 POUNDS PRESSURE. THEN TURN OFF THE HEAT AND THE FOOD INSIDE WILL REMAIN PRESERVED UNTIL YOU OPEN THE COOKER.

Bow Bender Delight

Serves: 2
Prep Time: 1½ hours

>   1 **lb. venison loin**
>   **butter**
>   1 **bell pepper, chopped**
>   1 **white onion, chopped**
>   4 **oz. mushrooms**
>   5 **dashes minced garlic**
>   ¼ **cup water**
>   **salt and pepper, to taste**

Cut loin into small steaks ¼- to ½-inch thick. Brown in butter on high heat setting. Reduce heat. Add balance of ingredients and simmer for one hour.

Jack Finklea
Ilion, New York

Barbecue Venison Chops

Serves: 4
Prep Time: 45 minutes

> 20 **venison chops**
>   6 **oz. beer**
>   1 **lg. onion, chopped**
>   4 **pats of butter**
>   2 **oz. garlic salt**

Place aluminum foil on hot grill with sides folded up, so there is no runoff of juices. Place chops on foil. Add beer, chopped onion and butter. Sprinkle garlic salt on chops each time you turn them. When chops are done, remove foil from grill. Place chops back on grill and sprinkle with garlic salt each time you turn them until charcoal black.

David Worrell
Vincentown, New Jersey

Venison Brochettes

Serves: 6
Prep Time: 30 minutes

> **6 venison cutlets, ½-inch thick**
> **6 green onions, chopped**
> **8 oz. whipped cream cheese**
> **6 slices bacon**

Place the cutlet between waxed paper and pound it thin with a mallet or flat side of a cleaver. It should be about ⅛-inch thick. Chop the green onions and mix them with the cream cheese. Spread the mixture over the cutlet and roll the cutlet up. Wrap a slice of the bacon around each one and place them in a baking pan seam side down. Bake at 350 degrees for 30 minutes. Don't be concerned if some of the filling cooks out. Next, turn on the broiler to brown the bacon. This should only take a couple of minutes. Serve with a dry wine and crusty Italian or French bread.

Gene Leone
Walnut Creek, California

SEEMS TO REMOVE THAT "WILD" TASTE IN BROILED STEAKS!

Venison Marinade

Serves: 3-4
Prep Time: 24 hours

> **1-1½ lbs. venison, sliced or cubed**
> **¼ cup soy sauce**
> **½ cup water**
> **1½ tsp. MSG**
> **½ tsp. pepper**
> **3 T. sugar**

Mix ingredients together. Pour over meat. Refrigerate at least 24 hours. Can marinate 3-4 days. Broil or barbecue.

John Sklba
Merrill, Michigan

Crab Apple Venison Roast

Serves: 4-8
Prep Time: 30 minutes

- **4-6 lb. venison roast**
- **1 tsp. salt**
- **1 T. pepper**
- **½ lb. bacon slices**
- **1 cup orange juice**
- **½ cup lemon juice**
- **¼ T. allspice**
- **½ cup butter**
- **½ cup crab apple jelly**

Season roast with salt and pepper. Cover with bacon slices. Sear meat at 450 degrees for 15 minutes. Reduce heat to 250 degrees for another 15 minutes per pound of roast. Baste frequently with a blend of ½ cup orange juice and allspice. About 30 minutes before roast is done, remove bacon. Make glaze from butter, ½ cup orange juice and crab apple jelly. Continue basting meat with glaze, uncover until done.

Irene Stocksdale
Dale City, Virginia

GRATING LEMON OR ORANGE PEEL—TO GRATE LEMON OR ORANGE PEEL, WASH AND DRY THE FRUIT. RUB IT, USING SHORT STROKES, ACROSS A SMALL SECTION OF A FINE GRATER. GRATE ONLY THE COLORED PART OF THE PEEL - THE WHITE PART HAS A BITTER TASTE. YOU WILL GET ABOUT 1 TABLESPOON OF GRATED LEMON RIND FROM A MEDIUM LEMON, AND 2 TABLESPOONS OF GRATED ORANGE PEEL FROM A MEDIUM ORANGE.

Cranberry Pot Roast

Serves: 6-8
Prep Time: 7½ hours

CHUCK OR RUMP IS BEST!

- 4 lbs. venison roast
- 2 cups cranberry juice cocktail
- flour for dredging
- salt and pepper
- 2 T. cooking oil
- 1 can whole cranberry sauce
- 1 garlic clove, minced
- ¼ tsp. powdered cloves
- 1 onion, sliced

Marinate venison in cranberry juice for 4 hours. Save marinade. Dust meat with flour, salt and pepper. Brown well on all sides in hot oil in a heavy kettle. Add whole cranberry sauce, 1 cup marinade, garlic, powdered cloves, onion and cover. Simmer 3½ hours or until tender. Skim fat from gravy. Thicken pan juices if desired.

Wyatt Coughlan
Acton, Massachusetts

FRUITS AND VEGETABLES THAT KEEP—FRESH FRUITS AND VEGETABLES THAT KEEP WELL ON BACKPACKING/HUNTING TRIPS ARE POTATOES, ONIONS, GARLIC, CUCUMBERS, YAMS, CABBAGE, CARROTS, APPLES, ORANGES AND LEMONS.

Frannie's Venison Roast Sauce

Serves: 4-6
Prep Time: 3½ hours

- **3-4 lb. venison roast**
- **4 carrots, diced**
- **4 med. potatoes, diced**
- **1 8-oz. can tomatoes**
- **3 T. brown sugar**
- **1 T. mustard**
- **3 T. Worcestershire sauce**
- **1 T. soy sauce**
- **½ tsp. pepper**
- **¼ tsp. salt**
- **¼ cup honey**
- **1 tsp. Tabasco**
- **½ tsp. onion powder**
- **½ tsp. garlic powder**

Place roast in foil-covered pan. Arrange cut carrots and potatoes. Combine remaining ingredients in a blender. Pour sauce over roast. Cover with foil and cook for three hours at 325 degrees.

Frances Houseal
Midland, Michigan

PLANT FOOD—A COUPLE OF PLANTS SITTIN' AROUND ARE NICE TO HAVE IN THE CABIN. THEY DRINK UP LEFTOVER COLD COFFEE AND COLD TEA, TOO.

Stuffed Neck Roast

Serves: 6-8
Prep Time: 3½ hours

  1 lg. venison neck
1½ loaves of dried bread
  1 tsp. salt
½ tsp. pepper
  3 eggs
  2 onions, chopped
    water
  2 tsp. sage

Bone large neck. Leave open and salt and pepper well. Let stand for ½ hour to let salt and pepper work in. In large mixing bowl or pan, make dressing by breaking up dry bread, adding 1 teaspoon salt and ½ teaspoon pepper, eggs, chopped onions, enough water to moisten well. Add 2 teaspoons sage. Test to see if it is enough. Add more sage if needed.

Lay neck roast in baking pan. Spread half of dressing on it. Then roll it up like a jellyroll. Put remaining dressing around roast and cover. Bake at 350 degrees for 2½ hours.

Fred Woods
Mancelona, Michigan

CAKED BAKING POWDER—IF YOUR BAKING POWDER IS CAKED, MOISTURE HAS GOTTEN IN AND IT HAS LOST ITS LEAVENING POWER. DON'T TAKE A CHANCE ON SPOILING A RECIPE AND WASTING OTHER INGREDIENTS. THROW OUT THE OLD CAN AND BUY A FRESH ONE.

Venison Roast

Serves: 2-4
Prep Time: 25 hours

> 1 lb. venison roast
> ⅔ cup dry red wine
> ⅓ cup water
> pepper
> bay leaves
> thyme
> mustard seed
> 1 lg. onion, sliced
> 1 garlic clove, sliced
> salt
> 1 cup currant jelly
> ½ cup sour cream
> 1 T. brandy

Marinate roast in mixture of wine, water, pepper, bay leaves, thyme, mustard seed and onion for 24 hours. After marinating, insert slices of garlic in roast. Rub roast with salt. Bake at 350 degrees. Baste with marinade drippings until roast is brown and tender. Place roast on hot platter. Add currant jelly, sour cream and brandy to drippings. Stir over high heat until mixture thickens. Garnish roast with orange strips or slices, and sliced pears.

Alex Carter
Alma, Georgia

SPICE UP SOUPS—TO SEASON SOUPS MAKE A BOUQUET GARNI BY PLACING PARSLEY, CELERY LEAVES, DILL, PEPPERCORNS, THYME AND BAY LEAF ON A SMALL SQUARE OF CHEESECLOTH. BRING CORNERS TOGETHER AND TIE SECURELY WITH A STRING. ADD TO SOUP KETTLE.

Roast Venison

Serves: several
Prep Time: 2 hours

1 7 lb. venison roast
10 larding strips
2 thinly sliced garlic bows
4 T. flour
salt and pepper to taste
1 stick butter, softened
1 tsp. thyme
1 tsp. rosemary
2½ cups beef stock

Using a larding needle, poke the larding strips into the roast in about 10 places, 1½ inches deep, following with a slice of garlic in each hole. If you don't have a larding needle you can put small squares of bacon or salt pork with a slice of garlic between on the meat top and bottom. Hold them in place with toothpicks. Mix salt and pepper with flour. Rub all meat surfaces with butter and dust with flour and herbs. Roast uncovered in roasting pan with ½ cup stock at 325 degrees for about two hours. Venison should be served rare but not bloody, so figure on a little over 15 minutes per pound. You may turn the oven to 400 degrees the last 10 to 12 minutes to brown the meat. Remove the meat from the pan, but keep it hot. Take the pan and mix in the remaining flour, stirring thoroughly. Place the pan over the heat to brown the flour and dredges. Stir in the stock and more water if necessary to make the gravy the desired thickness.

Tom Squier
Aberdeen, North Carolina

FOR EASIER CAMP COOKING—PACKAGE THE DRY INGREDIENTS FOR A MEAL IN A ZIP-LOCK PLASTIC BAG AND ADD THE LIQUIDS IN CAMP.

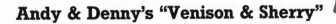

Andy & Denny's "Venison & Sherry"

Serves: several
Prep Time: overnight plus 2½ hours

> **4-5 lb. roast**
> **1 T. salt**
> **1 cup apple cider vinegar**
> **2 T. mixed pickling spices**
> **½ cup water**
> **salt and pepper**
> **garlic salt**
> **seasoned salt**
> **5 strips bacon, cut in halves**
> **2 med. onions, sliced**
> **3 cups water**
> **6 beef bouillon cubes**
> **2 T. cornstarch**
> **⅓ cup water**
> **½ cup cooking sherry**

The night before roasting, place roast in a large pot and cover with water. Add 1 tablespoon salt, 1 cup apple cider vinegar and 2 tablespoons mixed pickling spices. Cover the pot and let stand overnight. (Roast can be frozen or thawed.)

Preheat oven at 350 degrees. Rinse off roast from the marinade pot and discard the rest of the marinade as this will no longer be needed. Place the roast in roaster and add ½ cup water to the bottom. Moderately season with salt, pepper, garlic salt and seasoned salt. Lay cut strips of bacon over roast and sliced onions. Cook until tender. Roast usually takes about 2 hours or a little longer.

When roast is done, remove and place on a platter, cover with foil and let cool. Save pan drippings. Leave onions and bacon strips in drippings for flavor.

To make gravy, add to the pan drippings 3 cups of water and 6 beef boullion cubes. Bring drippings to a boil and dissolve the cubes stirring constantly. In a shaker, put 2 heaping tablespoons of cornstarch with ⅓ cup of water. Cap and shake until dissolved and milky. Reduce the heat on the already boiling drippings and slowly add to the pan drippings, stirring. Repeat the cornstarch step until desired thickness.

Remove gravy from heat and add ½ cup of cooking sherry, blending with the gravy mixture. Slice the roast in thin to medium slices and return to the gravy and sherry mixture. You may add fresh sliced or canned mushrooms (drained) while making the gravy if desired. Serve over mashed potatoes, rice or noodles or make hot roast venison sandwiches with kaiser rolls or buns.

Dennis Fenske
Brook Park, Ohio

San Gabriel Roast Venison

Serves: 6
Prep Time: 3-3½ hours

> **4-5 lb. venison roast**
> **¼ cup oil**
> **sage**
> **garlic clove, sliced**
> **salt**
> **fresh ground pepper**
> **¼ lb. salt pork, diced**
> **2 med. onions, chopped**
> **2 garlic cloves, minced**
> **1 bay leaf**
> **3 carrots**
> **1 leek**
> **2 cups beef stock or bouillon**

Rub meat with oil, sage and garlic. Sprinkle with salt and pepper. Cook salt pork over moderate heat until crisp and brown. Remove pork bits. Brown meat on all sides in hot fat. Reduce heat and add onions, garlic, bay leaf, carrots, leek and beef stock. Cover tightly until meat is tender, 2½ to 3 hours.

Place meat and vegetables on platter and thicken liquid as desired for gravy.

Alan Conzelmann
Arcadia, California

Crock Pot Barbecue

Serves: 6-8
Prep Time: 8-12 hours

CAN BE USED WITH ANY RED MEAT. JUST CUT IN 1-INCH CUBES!

- 3 lbs. venison stew meat
- 1 cup onion, diced
- 4-5 garlic cloves, chopped
- 1 cup red wine vinegar
- ½ cup Worcestershire sauce
- 2 tsp. Lawrey's Natural Choice seasoning for meat
- 2 tsp. seasoned salt
- 1 lb. bacon
- 2 cups catsup
- ½ cup molasses
- ½ cup brown sugar

Place meat, onion, garlic, vinegar, Worcestershire sauce and seasoning in crock pot. Cook on high for 1 to 2 hours until meat is cooked. Cook bacon and crumble or chop. Add bacon, catsup, molasses and brown sugar. Turn crockpot on low and heat for the rest of the day. Serve over rice, potatoes or toast.

Barak Capron
Cheyenne, Wyoming

TWO BAGS ARE BETTER THAN ONE—TO MARINATE MEAT USE TWO JUMBO PLASTIC FOOD-STORAGE BAGS. PLACE MEAT AND MARINADE IN ONE BAG, TIE OR ZIP-LOCK AND PLACE IN THE OTHER BAG. CLOSE THAT BAG TIGHT AND THE MEAT CAN BE TURNED EASILY, WITHOUT MAKING A MESS.

Mush & Meat

Serves: varies
Prep Time: 45 minutes

12 oz. cubed venison
**   bacon drippings**
2 quarts water
1 T. salt
2 cups yellow corn meal

Put meat in a frying pan and fry it with bacon fat. In a pot, add 2 quarts of water. Let boil and add salt. Add the corn meal, a cup at a time, into the pot and stir continuously. Add the meat, stirring until thick.

Rick Sinchak
Warren, Ohio

Sage Of The Ozark's Supper

Serves: 6-8
Prep Time: 2 hours

3 lbs. venison stew meat
4 cups water
2 tsp. parsley, chopped
1 cup catsup
5 T. bacon drippings
1 tsp. paprika
½ cup flour
½ cup red wine
½ lb. green beans, cut up

Place the stew meat in a large pot and add water. Simmer for 75 minutes. Then drain ½ of the water out. Add remaining ingredients. Mix well. Simmer for 45 minutes. Stir frequently. Serve with hot corn bread.

Rick Sinchak
Warren, Ohio

Gordon's Venison Stew

Serves: 8
Prep Time: 3½ hours

- **2½ lbs. venison, cut in 1½-inch cubes**
- **⅓ cup flour**
- **⅓ cup salad oil**
- **1 cup onion, chopped**
- **1 garlic clove, minced**
- **3 cups water**
- **1 tsp. salt**
- **½ cup Worcestershire sauce**
- **¼ tsp. pepper**
- **4 beef bouillon cubes**
- **5 med. potatoes**
- **1 16-oz. bag carrots, cut up**
- **1 10-oz. package peas**

About 3½ hours before serving, coat meat with flour and brown
in oil. Remove from pan. Add onions and garlic. Cook until
tender. Gradually stir in water, salt, Worcestershire sauce,
pepper and bouillon. Return meat. Simmer 2½ hours. Add
potatoes and carrots. Simmer 20 minutes. Stir in peas. Cover.
Simmer 5 to 10 minutes until vegetables are tender. Add a little
flour and water to thicken if you like your stew thick.

Gordon Zurn
Waubun, Minnesota

CAKE DOESN'T STICK—SIFT POWDERED SUGAR OVER A CAKE
PLATE BEFORE YOU PUT YOUR CAKE ON IT TO FROST, THEN IT WON'T
STICK TO THE PLATE WHEN SERVED.

Tom's Venison Stew

Serves: 5-6
Prep Time: 2¼ hours

>   2 **lbs. venison, cubed**
> **¼ cup flour**
>   1 **tsp. salt**
> **¼ tsp. pepper**
>   3 **T. oil**
>   2 **tsp. beef bouillon**
>   2 **onions, cut up**
>   1 **stalk celery, diced**
>   1 **bay leaf**
>   3 **cups water**
>   2 **cups fresh mushrooms**
>   4 **potatoes, quartered**
>   4 **carrots, cut up**
>   2 **T. flour**
> **3¼ cups water**

In large bowl coat meat with flour, salt and pepper. In large
pot, brown meat in oil. Add bouillon, onions, celery, bay leaf
and 3 cups water. Simmer covered for 1½ hours, or until
tender. Remove bay leaf. Add mushrooms, potatoes and
carrots. Cover and continue cooking until vegetables are
tender, about 30 to 45 minutes. Combine 2 tablespoons flour
and ¼ cup water. Stir into stew juices. Heat until thick. Stir
constantly.

Thomas Bruni
Fond du Lac, Wisconsin

PRESSURE COOKER IS QUICK—ALTHOUGH LARGER AND
HEAVIER TO CARRY THAN MOST COOKING PANS, A PRESSURE COOKER
COMES IN HANDY TO QUICKLY PREPARE FOODS ON HUNTING TRIPS.

Onion Stew With Venison

Serves: 4-6
Prep Time: 2 hours and 40 minutes

   3 **lbs. venison**
   4 **T. butter**
   3 **oz. tomato paste**
   1 **garlic clove, chopped**
   1 **bay leaf**
1-2 **T. wine vinegar**
    salt and pepper
    water
   2 **lbs. sm. white onions**
   1 **cup walnut halves**
    feta cheese (optional)

Cut meat into 1-inch cubes and brown in butter in casserole.
Add tomato paste, garlic, bay leaf, wine vinegar, salt, pepper
and enough water to cover. Bring to a boil. Cover tightly and
simmer for 1½ to 2 hours or until tender. Remove meat from
casserole and add white onions to sauce remaining in
casserole. Bring to a boil again, cover and simmer for 20
minutes or until onions are cooked. Return meat to casserole.
Add walnut halves and continue to simmer for 15 to 20 minutes.
During last 5 minutes of cooking add cubes of feta cheese
(optional).

Steve Stathopoulos
Montreal, Quebec

PEELING GARLIC CLOVES—AN EASY WAY TO PEEL A CLOVE OF
GARLIC IS TO CRUSH IT LIGHTLY WITH THE FLAT SIDE OF A LARGE KNIFE
AND THE SKIN WILL SEPARATE.

Venison-Beef Stew

Serves: 4-6
Prep Time: 2½ hours

  1 **lb. venison**
  1 **lb. beef**
     Adolph's meat tenderizer
     water
  2 **7.6-oz. cans stew starter**
  3-4 **carrots, chopped**
  1 **8.5-oz. can sweet peas**
  1 **med. onion, diced**
  4-5 **med. potatoes, diced**
  3-4 **celery stalks, chopped**
  4 **T. butter**
  1-2 **beef bouillon cubes**
  1 **bay leaf**
  2 **tsp. Kitchen Bouquet**
  1 **garlic clove, minced**
  1 **tsp. Worcestershire sauce**

Cut up venison and beef into bite size pieces. Sprinkle with
Adolph's meat tenderizer. Let set for 10 minutes; then brown
meat. Add water and rest of ingredients and bring to a boil.
Reduce heat, cover and simmer for 1½ hours or until meat and
vegetables are tender. Use large 4-quart pot.

Alfred Ingalls
Pittsfield, New Hampshire

TO KEEP HERBS—CHOP FRESH HERBS WHEN THEY'RE AVAILABLE
AND FREEZE THEM IN SMALL PLASTIC BAGS OR CONTAINERS FOR USE IN
YOUR RECIPES YEAR-ROUND.

Venison Stew & Dumplings

Serves: 4-6
Prep Time: 3-5 hours

> 5 lbs. venison, cut in 1-inch cubes
> 4 quarts water
> 1 onion, diced
> garlic
> salt and pepper
> meat tenderizer
> celery salt
> 6-8 potatoes, diced
> 2 cans stewed tomatoes
> 1 lg. can tomato juice or V-8
> 1 bag frozen vegetables
> dumplings, made from Bisquick

EXCELLENT FOR THOSE WHO CLAIM THEY DON'T LIKE VENISON!

In 8-quart pan put diced venison in 4 quarts water and onion. Add desired seasoning. Bring to boil and cover. Boil about 30 to 45 minutes. Add potatoes and tomato products. Bring to boil again, about 30 minutes. Keep covered. Add vegetables. After meat, potatoes and vegetables are done, turn down to simmer. The longer it simmers the better it is. About 1 hour before serving time, mix and add dumplings according to package. Serve when dumplings are done.

William Parker
Genoa, Wisconsin

TOMATO SEED REMOVAL—TO REMOVE SEEDS FROM A TOMATO, SLICE THE TOMATO IN HALF AND GENTLY SQUEEZE IT UNTIL THE SEEDS FALL OUT.

Wild Harry's Stew

Serves: 4
Prep Time: 12 hours

    1-2 lbs. venison
      4 cups water
      1 pkg. stew seasoning
      1 jar salsa   ←   *SECRET IS IN THE SALSA!*
    4-5 lg. potatoes
    6-7 pieces celery
    4-5 lg. carrots
      1 sm. onion

Using at least a 3-quart crockpot, put water, seasoning and salsa into pot and start cooking. Cut potatoes, celery, carrots and onions in bite size pieces. Add to pot. Cut venison in bite size pieces, remembering to cut off all fat. Place in crock pot and let cook on high for at least 8 hours.

Lloyd Crawford
Centralia, Washington

Country Style Venison Stew

Serves: 6-8
Prep Time: 6-8 hours

  2½ lbs. venison, cubed
    2 cans mushroom soup
    1 pkg. dry onion soup mix
    1 lg. can of sliced mushrooms
    1 T. butter
    1 tsp. salt
    ¼ tsp. pepper

Cube 2½ lbs. venison. Add to crock pot. Add the rest of the ingredients and cook on high for 30 minutes. Reduce to low and simmer 6 to 8 hours.

James Smith
Staunton, Virginia

Mar's Venison Stew

Serves: 4
Prep Time: 8 hours

- **2 lbs. venison, cubed**
- **1 lg. onion, diced**
- **1 garlic clove, diced**
- **1 can drained potatoes, diced**
- **4 fresh carrots, diced**
- **1 cup corn**
- **1 cup peas**
- **1 celery stalk, diced**
- **2 oz. Marsala wine (optional)**
- **1 tsp. salt and pepper**
- **1 tsp. cornstarch**

Fill crockpot half full of water. Add venison, onion, garlic, potatoes, carrots, corn, peas, celery, Marsala, salt and pepper. Stir in cornstarch. If needed, add an extra cup of water. Cover. Cook on low heat for eight hours.

Dan Zawidski
Reading, Pennsylvania

CREATE A RICHER CHICKEN STOCK—TO MAKE CANNED CHICKEN STOCK RICHER BOIL IT WITH INEXPENSIVE PARTS OF CHICKEN SUCH AS BACKS AND NECKS, A CUT UP ONION, A PEELED AND CUT UP CARROT, A FEW SPRIGS OF PARSLEY AND SEVERAL PEPPERCORNS. STRAIN AND USE THE STOCK FOR SOUPS AND STEWS.

Venison Swiss Stew

Serves: 6
Prep Time: 20 minutes

1½ lbs. venison, cubed
½ cup flour
1 tsp. salt
¼ tsp. pepper
3 T. shortening
1 lg. onion, chopped
1 lg. can of tomatoes
1 green pepper, chopped

EXCELLENT SERVED OVER RICE!

Dredge venison in mixture of flour, salt and pepper. Heat shortening until foamy. Add meat and cook until brown on one side. Turn and add onion. Continue cooking. Add tomatoes and green pepper. Cover, reduce heat and cook 1 to 2 hours.

James Smith
Staunton, Virginia

Deer Stew

Serves: 4-6 people
Prep Time: 11 hours

2 lbs. venison, cubed
flour
½ can corn
2 sliced carrots
½ can peas
½ can stew starter
1 can cream of mushroom soup
½ can sm. onions
2-3 cups water

Roll venison in flour and brown. Put all ingredients in a crock pot. Cook on high 2 to 3 hours, then low for 8 hours.

Jay Crawford
Weare, New Hampshire

Mountain Top Venison Stew

Serves: 2-4
Prep Time: 2½ hours

8 oz. venison ham, cubed
flour and/or saltine crackers
dash of meat tenderizer
salt, pepper and garlic to taste
½ onion, diced
1 tsp. Worcestershire sauce
1 tsp. catsup
1 tsp. instant coffee
1 16 oz. can red kidney beans
1 16 oz. can potatoes
1 16 oz. can sliced carrots
1 8 oz. can peas
¼ green pepper, diced

Cut venison into bite-size pieces and shake in mixture of
crushed crackers, flour, meat tenderizer, salt, pepper and
garlic salt. Brown meat in pot used to cook stew. Add water to
cover. Add onion, Worcestershire sauce, catsup and 1 teaspoon
instant coffee. Cover and cook on low heat for two hours. Add
kidney beans, potatoes, carrots, peas and green pepper. Cover
and cook on medium heat for 30 minutes. Add water as needed
for desired thickness. Serve over toast or with favorite bread.
(For camping, flour mixture can be prepared and then carried
in a ziplock bag.)

Russell Shoate
Glade Valley, North Carolina

PREPARE MEALS IN ADVANCE—BEFORE YOUR TRIP, PREPARE
AND PACKAGE YOUR MEALS AT HOME FOR QUICK PREPARATION IN CAMP.

Pie's Easy Oven Stew

Serves: 6
Prep Time: 4 hours

    2 lbs. venison stew meat
    1 lg. onion, chopped
    6 stalks celery, chopped
    6 carrots, sliced
    3 med. potatoes, diced
    1 tsp. seasoned salt
    1 tsp. pepper
    1 T. sugar
    3 T. quick cooking tapioca
 1½ cups tomato juice
    parsley flakes

USE ANY BIG GAME!

Mix raw meat and raw vegetables together and place into a
13x9-inch baking pan. Blend seasoned salt, pepper, sugar and
tapioca into the tomato juice and pour over the meat/vegetable
mixture. Sprinkle with parsley flakes. Cover tightly with tin foil
and bake at 250 degrees for 4 hours.

Mike Piaskowski
Green Bay, Wisconsin

MEAT SERVINGS PER POUND—GENERALLY, THE NUMBER OF
SERVINGS PER POUND ARE AS FOLLOWS:
1 POUND OF BONELESS MEAT—4 SERVINGS
1 POUND OF MEAT, FEW BONES—3 SERVINGS
1 POUND OF MEAT, MUCH BONE—2 SERVINGS

Venison Patties

Serves: several
Prep Time: ½ hour

- **1 lb. ground venison**
- **1 onion, minced**
- **½ tsp. grated lemon peel**
- **⅛ tsp. thyme**
- **⅛ tsp. garlic powder**
  bread crumbs
- **½ lb. bacon, chopped**
  salt and pepper to taste
- **⅛ tsp. marjoram**
- **1 egg**

Mix ingredients by hand adding enough bread crumbs to attain a firm consistency. Form into 3-inch roll. Cut into slices and fry.

Alfred Sabino
Ringwood, New Jersey

Berky's Barbecue Venison Burgers

Serves: 6
Prep Time: 1 hour

- **1 lb. ground venison**
- **½ lb. ground pork**
- **1 T. garlic powder**
- **1 T. onion powder**
- **1 tsp. pepper**
- **1 tsp. Accent**
- **½ cup water**
- **1 lg. bottle barbecue sauce**

Mix all ingredients together except for last two. Form into 6 patties. Brown in large skillet, drain grease and return to low heat. Add last two ingredients and simmer for 45 minutes.

Bill Berkant
Wilkesbarre, Pennsylvania

BBQ Venison

Serves: several
Prep Time: overnight (stock) plus 1 hour

5-15 lbs. venison, cubed
1 3-quart bottle ginger ale ← *SECRET IS GINGER ALE!*
2 cups venison stock

Venison Stock: Cover venison bones with water in a large pot and simmer until the meat will fall off. Allow to cool overnight and skim off hardened fat. Strip meat off bones and ladle meat and stock into loaf pans to freeze.

Cook venison meat in a covered roaster at 350 degrees for about one hour with the stock to keep it from sticking. Remove the lid, cover with ginger ale and continue cooking until tender. Shred meat with a potato masher, add catsup and commercial BBQ sauce to taste. Continue cooking until desired consistency is reached.

Eugene Halliwill
Ashland, Ohio

TO RID HANDS OF ODOR—AFTER CUTTING UP STRONG SMELLING INGREDIENTS SUCH AS ONIONS OR GARLIC RUB YOUR HANDS WITH CELERY SALT OR SEED AND RINSE WITH WATER. THE ODOR WILL BE GONE.

Venison Mincemeat

Serves: varies
Prep Time: 4 hours

    4 lbs. venison, trim fat
    3 lbs. apples, peeled and quartered
    3 lbs. raisins
    ¾ lb. beef suet
    1 T. cinnamon
    1 T. ground ginger
    1 T. ground cloves
    1 T. nutmeg
    1 tsp. allspice
    1 lb. brown sugar
    2 quarts cider

Cut meat in small pieces. Cover with water and simmer until done, about 1 to 2 hours. Cool to remove all fat from liquid. Grind apple and grind meat using coarse grinder. You should have about 2 quarts of ground meat. Combine all ingredients in a large kettle, simmer for 2 hours to blend flavors. Stir often to prevent sticking. Use as is for cookies, and add 1 cup chopped apples to every 2 cups mincemeat for pies. Makes about 10 quarts. If you are going to freeze it for more than a couple of months, leave out suet and add butter when using mincemeat.

Verne Turner
Fort Plain, New York

MAKE SURE YOU WRAP MEAT WELL—IF NOT PROPERLY WRAPPED FOR THE FREEZER, GAME WILL LOSE MOISTURE, BECOME DRY, TOUGH AND OFTEN STRINGY.

Venison Hash

Serves: 4-6
Prep Time: 1½ hours

> 1½ **lbs. ground venison**
>   3 **lg. onions, diced**
>   1 **lg. green pepper, diced**
>   1 **16-oz. can tomatoes**
>   2 **tsp. salt**
> ⅓ **tsp. pepper**
> 1½ **tsp. chili powder**
>   1 **sm. red pepper, diced**
> ½ **cup chopped chiles (optional)**

Preheat the oven to 350 degrees. In a large skillet cook and stir meat, onions, peppers until meat is brown and vegetables tender. Drain off the fat and stir in tomatoes, salt, pepper, chili powder, red pepper and optional chiles. Heat through and pour into a covered casserole dish. Bake one hour stirring a couple times while cooking.

Tom Squier
Aberdeen, North Carolina

MARINADES WORK BEST—HANGING GAME DOESN'T TENDERIZE IT; RATHER, IT ENHANCES THE "WILD GAME" FLAVOR. MARINADES TENDERIZE.

Hamburger Rice Pie

Serves: 4-6
Prep Time: 1 hour

    1 lb. ground venison, browned and drained
    ½ cup bread crumbs
    ¼ cup green pepper, chopped
    ¼ cup onion, chopped
    1½ cans tomato sauce
    2½ cups cooked rice
    ½ cup grated cheese (your choice)
    salt and pepper to taste

Combine venison, bread crumbs, green pepper, onion and ½ can tomato sauce in a large pie shell. Then mix rice, cheese, salt and pepper and 1 can tomato sauce. Place this mixture on top of first mixture and spread other half can of tomato sauce over top. Bake in a pie pan at 375 degrees for about 35 minutes.

Bobby Wright
Highland, Indiana

ONIONS AND POTATOES DON'T MIX—DO NOT STORE ONIONS WITH POTATOES. ONIONS RELEASE A GAS THAT HASTENS SPOILAGE OF POTATOES.

Venison Burger Bake

Serves: 4-6
Prep Time: 45 minutes

  1 **lb. ground venison**
  2 **cups Jiffy baking mix**
  ½ **cup milk**
  1 **can cream of mushroom soup**
  ¼ **cup milk**
1½ **cups cabbage, shredded**
  ½ **onion, diced**
  1 **cup broccoli, diced**

Fry venison and set aside. Make a dough of baking mix and milk. Spread ½ of dough in greased pie plate. Mix cooked venison, soup and milk and pour into pie plate. Sprinkle with cabbage, onion and broccoli. Top with other ½ of dough. Bake at 400 degrees for 20 to 30 minutes.

Rex Morgan
Kansas City, Missouri

ADD A LITTLE TABASCO—ADD TABASCO TO A RECIPE AT THE END OF COOKING BECAUSE IF COOKED TOO LONG IT BECOMES BITTER TASTING.

Venison SOS

Serves: 4
Prep Time: 30 minutes

 2 **lbs. ground venison**
 2 **T. oil**
 1 **sm. can mushrooms**
 1 **can mushroom soup**
 ¾ **cup onion, chopped**
 1 **green pepper, chopped**
 1 **garlic clove, minced**
 1 **tsp. oregano**
 1 **tsp. parsley flakes**
 ½ **tsp. salt**
   pepper

In large skillet, brown meat in oil. Add mushrooms and simmer.
Drain off all liquids and stir in soup. Simmer until soup is
blended into meat. Add onion, green pepper and garlic. Saute
until soft. Add oregano, parsley, salt and pepper to taste.

Karl Wells
Carrollton, Ohio

USE BREAD WHILE BROILING—WHEN BROILING MEAT IN THE OVEN PUT ONE OR TWO PIECES OF DRIED BREAD IN THE BOTTOM OF THE PAN. THE BREAD WILL SOAK UP EXCESS FAT AND CUT DOWN ON SMOKING OR POSSIBLE FIRES.

Venison Cacciatore

Serves: 4
Prep Time: 45 minutes

> 2 **lbs. venison**
> 4 **slices bacon, cut up**
> 1 **lg. onion, diced**
> 2 **garlic cloves, diced**
> **bacon grease**
> 2 **oz. Marsala wine**
> 16 **oz. can stewed tomatoes, crushed**
> 1 **tsp. cornstarch**
> 2 **cups cooked rice**

In skillet, fry bacon. Add diced onion, diced garlic and cook until clear. In separate skillet, cook venison in bacon grease until done.

Drain venison and add to skillet with onions, garlic and bacon. To this add Marsala and stewed tomatoes, crushing them with a spoon into chunks. Do not drain. Stir in cornstarch and simmer 15 minutes. Place cooked rice on plate and spoon cacciatore over the top.

Dan Zawidski
Reading, Pennsylvania

FOR FRESHER WATER—TO KEEP WATER FRESH LONGER WHEN BACKPACKING OR CAMPING, ADD A SLICED WHOLE LEMON TO A GALLON OF WATER.

Sandra's Saucy Venison

Serves: 4
Prep Time: 45 minutes

**1½ lbs. venison, cubed
flour
½ cup oil
1 tsp. onion, minced
1 T. parsley flakes
1 sm. jar spaghetti sauce**

Coat venison in flour and fry in oil. Add minced onion and
parsley flakes as it cooks. Drain on paper towel when done and
discard all but 1 or 2 tablespoons oil. Return venison to skillet
and add spaghetti sauce. Simmer 20 minutes.

Sandra Crummett
Sugar Grove, West Virginia

Venison In Casserole

Serves: 2-4
Prep Time: 1 hour

**1 lb. venison roast, cut up
2 T. olive oil
2 T. butter
2 T. flour
1 can mushrooms
1 tsp. salt
1 T. onion
½ tsp. black pepper
1 T. parsley
pinch of cayenne
1 pint of meat stock**

Brown venison in olive oil and butter. Add all ingredients and
simmer for 1 hour.

Alex Carter
Alma, Georgia

Pie's Venison Tip

Serves: 6-8
Prep Time: 1½ hours

>   2 **lbs. venison stew meat**
>   1 **cup flour**
>   1 **tsp. seasoned salt**
>   ½ **tsp. pepper**
>   ¼ **cup oil**
>   1 **lg. onion, chopped**
>   1 **4-oz can mushroom stems & pieces, drained**
>   1 **8-oz. can sliced water chestnuts, drained**
>   4 **stalks celery, chopped**
>   6 **carrots, sliced**
>   2 **T. Lea & Perrins English pub mustard**
>   6 **beef bouillon cubes, dissolved in 1 cup hot**
>   **water**
> 6-8 **servings egg noodles**

Combine flour, seasoned salt and pepper. Coat meat and
brown in hot cooking oil. Mix in the onions, mushrooms, water
chestnuts, celery and carrots and brown slightly. Let sit on low
heat while you mix the mustard and bouillon together. Pour this
over the meat/vegetable mixture and bring to a boil. Lower
heat and simmer, covered, until the celery and carrots are
tender, approximately 1 hour. Cook egg noodles according to
package directions. Thicken meat mixture with remaining flour
if desired.

Mike Piaskowski
Green Bay, Wisconsin

FOR BEST GARLIC TASTE—COOK GARLIC ONLY UNTIL IT IS
GOLDEN. WHEN IT IS BROWNED OR BURNED IT DEVELOPS A BITTER
TASTE.

Venison Parmigiana

Serves: 6
Prep Time: 45 minutes

8-10 venison cutlets, sliced thin
1 egg, beaten
2 cups bread crumbs
2 T. butter
1 lb. mozzarella cheese, sliced
1 jar tomato sauce
salt and pepper to taste
¼ tsp. basil
¼ tsp. oregano
2 garlic cloves, sliced thin

MOM'S HOMEMADE SAUCE WORKS WELL HERE!

Pound sliced venison between sheets of waxed paper until
very thin. Dip slices in beaten egg and then into bread crumbs
until covered. Pan fry briefly in butter until golden brown.
Place in baking pan and cover with mozzarella slices and
tomato sauce. Sprinkle spices and garlic around evenly. Bake
10 to 12 minutes at 350 degrees. Serve with favorite pasta.

Alfred Sabino
Ringwood, New Jersey

APPLES AND CARROTS DON'T MIX—DO NOT STORE APPLES WITH CARROTS. APPLES RELEASE A GAS THAT GIVES CARROTS A BITTER TASTE.

Hungry Boy Casserole

Serves: 4-6
Prep Time: 45 minutes

1½ lbs. ground venison
1 cup celery
½ cup onion, chopped
½ cup green pepper
1 can tomato soup
¼ cup water
1 tsp. salt
1 tsp. paprika
1 can pork and beans
1 container biscuits

Fry venison with celery, onion, green pepper. Add soup, water, salt, paprika, pork and beans. Place in casserole and put biscuits on top of meat mixture. Bake at 425 degrees for 25 to 30 minutes or until biscuits are golden brown.

Wayne Umlor
Conklin, Michigan

USE LESS DRIED HERBS—WHEN USING DRIED HERBS IN RECIPES, USE HALF AS MUCH AS YOU WOULD OF A FRESH HERB.

Venison Jambalaya

Serves: 5-6
Prep Time: 1 hour

- **2 lbs. venison meat, diced**
- **½ lb. bacon**
- **2 med. onions, chopped**
- **2 ribs celery, chopped**
- **1 cup parsley, chopped**
- **1 med. bell pepper, chopped**
- **1 tsp. garlic powder**
- **½ cup green onion tops, chopped**
- **salt**
- **Chinese red pepper**
- **8 cups water**
- **2 tsp. Kitchen Bouquet**
- **4 cups long grain rice**

Brown ½ lb. bacon until crisp in a heavy 6-quart pot. Remove the bacon, crumble and set aside. Leave the drippings in the pot. Saute onions until dark golden brown. Add celery, parsley, bell pepper, garlic powder and onion tops. Cook for about 10 minutes. Sprinkle in salt and Chinese red pepper to taste. Add water, Kitchen Bouquet and reserved bacon bits. Toss in venison meat as soon as the mixture begins to boil. Cook over medium heat for 10 minutes, then add the rice. Cook for another 10 minutes and then cover and cook until rice is tender. Stir once to allow juices to spread evenly throughout.

Mary Smith
Lewiston, Minnesota

BRUSH YOUR VEGETABLES—USE A CLEAN, STIFF TOOTHBRUSH AS A VEGETABLE BRUSH.

Stuffed Cabbage With Venison

Serves: 6-8
Prep Time: 3 hours

1½ lbs. ground venison
1 egg
⅓ cup rice
1 onion, chopped
Small amount of milk
salt and pepper
1 head cabbage
1 can sauerkraut
1 can tomato sauce
1 can tomatoes

Mix meat, egg, rice and onion together. Add milk until rice is moist. Add salt and pepper. Cut core out of cabbage and place cabbage in boiling water until leaves are soft. Roll meat mixture in each leaf of cabbage. Put ½ can sauerkraut in bottom of roaster and put rolls on top. Put rest of sauerkraut on top of rolls. Chop rest of cabbage and put on top of sauerkraut. Add tomato sauce and tomatoes (breaking up tomatoes). Add a little water. Bake at 325 degrees for 2 to 2½ hours.

Richard James
Berlin Heights, Ohio

CHECK PRODUCE DAILY—PRODUCE WILL LAST LONGER IF YOU SPEND A FEW MINUTES DAILY CHECKING FOR SPOILAGE SPOTS AND CUTTING IT.

Dr. Z Lasagna

Serves: 6
Prep Time: 2½ hours

- 1 lb. venison sausage, spicy
- 2 tsp. onion salt
- 2 tsp. garlic salt
- 1 16-oz. can whole tomatoes
- 1 15-oz. can tomato sauce
- 3 T. dried parsley flakes
- 1 tsp. sugar
- 1 tsp. basil leaves
- 2 tsp. salt
- 1 8-oz. can mushroom pieces
- 6 uncooked lasagna noodles
- 1 16-oz. package ricotta cheese
- ½ cup Parmesan cheese
- 1½ tsp. oregano leaves
- 2 cups shredded mozzarella cheese

Cook and stir sausage, onion and garlic salt in 10-inch skillet until sausage is light brown. Drain. Add tomatoes (with liquid), tomato sauce, 2 tablespoons parsley, sugar, basil, ½ teaspoon salt and mushrooms. Heat to boil, stirring occasionally. Reduce heat. Simmer uncovered until mixture is consistency of thick spaghetti sauce, about 1 hour.

Cook noodles as directed on package. Reserve ½ cup of the sauce mixture. Mix ricotta cheese, ¼ cup Parmesan, 1 tablespoon parsley, 1½ teaspoons salt and oregano. Layer ⅓ each of the noodles, remaining sauce mixture, mozzarella cheese and ricotta cheese mixture in ungreased oblong pan, 10x6x2 inches. Repeat above process until you have 2 layers. Spoon reserve sauce on top, top with mozzarella and sprinkle with Parmesan. Cook uncovered at 350 degrees for 45 minutes. Let stand 15 minutes.

Donald Zander
Stanfield, Arizona

Venison Scallopini

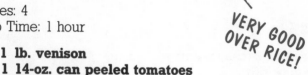

VERY GOOD OVER RICE!

Serves: 4
Prep Time: 1 hour

    1 lb. venison
    1 14-oz. can peeled tomatoes
    3 oz. tomato paste
    ½ green pepper, cut into small pieces
    1 med. onion, sliced
    ¼ tsp. garlic salt
    ½ tsp. basil
    ½ tsp. oregano
    ¼ cup sugar
    4 T. oil

Place tomatoes, tomato paste, green pepper, onion, spices and sugar in large covered skillet. Simmer over low heat for one hour. Meanwhile, cut venison into strips ⅛-inch thick, removing all fat and gristle. Flash fry venison in iron skillet in oil until slightly pink. Fry venison one layer at a time and turn individually. Drain on paper towels. Add meat to bubbling sauce just before serving.

Bruce Block
Mt. Laurel, New Jersey

DEGREASING SOUPS—SKIM THE SURFACE OF SOUPS OR STEWS AND THEN WRAP A FEW ICE CUBES IN HEAVY-WEIGHT PAPER TOWELS AND RUN THEM OVER THE TOP OF THE SOUP.

Venison Meat Pies

Serves: 6-8
Prep Time: 3½ hours

>   3 lg. venison steaks
>   4 med. potatoes
>   6 carrots
>   1 lg. onion
>   3 packages gravy mix
>   1 tsp. salt
>   ¼ tsp. pepper
>   dash Tabasco sauce
>   4 cups flour
>   2 tsp. salt
>   1⅓ cups shortening
> 12-14 T. cold water

Chop venison, potatoes, carrots and onions into small cubes.
Make gravy mix as directed. Simmer meat mixture in gravy
until tender, adding salt, pepper and a dash of Tabasco sauce.
Make a crumb mixture with a fork out of the flour, salt and
shortening. Stir in water to form a dough. Roll pie crust into four
6-inch rectangles. Stuff with meat mixture and pinch closed.
Bake at 350 degrees for 30 to 35 minutes. Serve hot.

Frances Houseal
Midland, Michigan

THE BEST BREAD—LOAF PANS OF GLASS, DARKENED METAL OR
DULL-FINISHED ALUMINUM ARE IDEAL FOR BAKING BREAD. THEY ABSORB
HEAT AND GIVE A NICE BROWN CRUST. TO DARKEN A SHINY TIN LOAF
PAN, HEAT IT FOR 5 HOURS IN A 350-DEGREE OVEN.

Microwave Shepherd's Pie

Serves: 4-6
Prep Time: 30 minutes

GREAT IF YOU'RE IN A HURRY!

1 lb. ground venison
1 med. onion, chopped
1 10-oz. pkg. frozen peas and carrots or green beans
1 10¾-oz. can tomato soup
1 tsp. Worcestershire sauce
½ tsp. salt
¼ tsp. basil
⅛ tsp. pepper
3 cups hot mashed potatoes
1 cup shredded cheddar cheese

Combine ground venison into a 2 quart casserole with the chopped onion. Microwave on high 4 to 6 minutes or until meat loses its pink color. Break up meat and drain off all grease. Microwave vegetables on high 2 to 3½ minutes or until well defrosted. Add tomato soup to meat and mix. Add all other items but the vegetables, potatoes and cheese. Mix well. Spread vegetables evenly over meat. Spread mashed potatoes over vegetables. Microwave on high for about 6 minutes and turn half way through cooking cycle. Spread cheese evenly over potatoes. You may use extra cheese if you wish. Microwave about 3 minutes and turn half way through this cycle. Let stand 5 minutes and serve. Can be reheated.

Bobby Wright
Highland, Indiana

SECRET FOR GREAT BISCUITS—TOO MUCH LIQUID MAKES THE DOUGH STICKY AND TOO LITTLE MAKES THE DOUGH COARSE AND DRY. FOLLOW RECIPE INSTRUCTIONS FOR PERFECT BISCUITS.

Tom's Venison Stroganoff

Serves: 5-6
Prep Time: 35 minutes

1½ lbs. venison, cubed
1 lb. fresh mushrooms
¾ cup butter
2 T. flour
2 cups beef bouillon
¼ cup pale dry sherry
1 tsp. dry mustard
1 lg. onion, sliced
⅔ cup sour cream

Saute mushrooms in ¼ cup butter until tender. Set aside. Add at least 1 tablespoon butter to pan. Add venison and brown. Set aside. If little butter remains, add 2 tablespoons butter and sprinkle in 2 tablespoons flour. Mix well. Slowly add 2 cups of beef bouillon. Stir well to form a smooth gravy. Add sherry and dry mustard. Blend well. Add the meat, mushrooms and onions. Simmer on low for 25 minutes. About 5 minutes before serving, add sour cream and blend well.

Thomas Bruni
Fond du Lac, Wisconsin

FLOUR AMOUNT MAY VARY—FLOUR TENDS TO DRY OUT DURING THE SUMMER MONTHS. IN THE FALL YOUR RECIPE MIGHT NOT NEED AS MUCH FLOUR AS IT DID IN THE SUMMER MONTHS.

Kyle's Venison Stroganoff

Serves: 4
Prep Time: 45 minutes

BEST OVER NOODLES OR RICE!

- **1 lb. venison stew meat**
- **4 T. butter or margarine**
- **8 oz. mushrooms, sliced**
- **2 med. onions, sliced**
- **1 garlic clove, finely chopped**
- **½ cup water**
- **1 tsp. instant beef bouillon**
- **1 tsp. salt**
- **1 tsp. pepper**
- **1 cup sour cream**
- **½ tsp. prepared mustard**

Heat 2 tablespoons butter in large skillet until melted. Add mushrooms, onions and garlic. Cover and simmer, stirring occasionally until onions are tender, 5 to 10 minutes. Remove vegetables and any liquid from skillet. Cook and stir stew meat in 2 tablespoons of butter over medium heat until browned, about 10 minutes. Add water, bouillon, salt and pepper. Heat to boiling, reduce heat. Cover and simmer until meat is desired tenderness, 10 to 15 minutes. Add vegetable mixture. Heat to boiling, reduce heat. Stir in sour cream and mustard. Heat until hot.

Kyle Geno
Dryden, Michigan

STORING CUT ONIONS—TO STORE HALF AN ONION, PLACE IT IN A JAR IN THE REFRIGERATOR. IT'LL STAY FRESH AND MOIST.

Corned Venison Reuben Bake

Serves: 4
Prep Time: 30 minutes

EVEN BETTER
REHEATED!

2 cups corned venison, diced or shredded
1 cup sauerkraut
1 cup Thousand Island dressing
2 cups shredded Swiss cheese
3 cups rye bread, diced

Mix all ingredients together adding bread last and turn into a
lightly greased baking dish (about 1½ inches deep). Bake at
350 degrees for 30 minutes, or until brown.

Eugene Halliwill
Ashland, Ohio

Green Pepper Deer Bake

Serves: 4
Prep Time: 2½ hours

2-2½ lbs. of venison, cubed
salt and pepper to taste
½ cup green pepper, chopped
1 cup onions, chopped
¼ cup celery, chopped fine
1 jar chili sauce
1 sauce jar of water

Place venison in baking dish, salt and pepper to taste. Cover
venison with green peppers, onion and celery. Cover this with
chili sauce and water. Bake covered for 2½ hours at 325
degrees. Serve on bed of rice.

Rick Cooper
Columbus, Indiana

Fricassee Of Venison

Serves: 6-8
Prep Time: 5-6 hours

> **2-3 lbs. venison, cubed**
>   **salt**
>   **2 T. garlic powder**
>   **1 T. oregano**
>   **1 cup Spanish olive oil**
>   **1 onion, diced**
>   **1 garlic clove, diced**
>   **1 T. cilantro**
>   **2 sm. cans tomato sauce**
>   **1 sm. can tomato paste**
>   **cooking wine**
>   **1 T. sugar (optional)**

Add first eight ingredients. Fry in skillet or pan for about 10 minutes until meat is brown. Then add tomato sauce, tomato paste and ½ bottle of cooking wine. Cook on low temperature for 5 or 6 hours. After 2 to 3 hours add other ½ bottle of cooking wine. If, toward the end, it tastes a little salty, add 1 tablespoon sugar, or as needed to give proper taste.

Manuel Nunez
Miami, Florida

SPIN THE EGG—IF YOU CAN'T REMEMBER WHICH EGGS IN THE REFRIGERATOR ARE HARD-BOILED AND WHICH ARE RAW, GIVE 'EM A SPIN. A HARD-BOILED EGG WILL SPIN LIKE A TOP, WHILE A RAW EGG WON'T SPIN AT ALL.

Warna's Venison Chili

Serves: 8-10
Prep Time: 3-4 hours

    2½ lbs. venison, coarsely ground
     2 T. vegetable oil
     1 lg. onion, chopped
     3 lg. garlic cloves, crushed
     2 T. Worcestershire sauce
     2 T. barbecue sauce
     2 T. chili powder
     1 T. brown sugar
     1 T. soy sauce
     1 4-oz. jar pimentos, chopped
     1 med. green pepper, diced
    ¼ cup celery, diced
     2 tsp. celery salt
     3 T. catsup
     1 tsp. ground cumin
     1 tsp. salt and pepper
     1 tsp. instant minced onion
     1 tsp. garlic powder
       dash red cayenne pepper
     1 15-oz. can stewed tomatoes
     2 T. jalapeno pepper juice (optional)

In 5-quart saucepot over medium heat, combine all ingredients
and cook for 3 to 4 hours. If you like spicy and hot, add 2 T. of
jalapeno pepper juice.

Warna Miller Reed
Matherville, Illinois

BROWN SUGAR—SOFTEN THE LUMPS IN BROWN SUGAR BY PUTTIN'
IT IN A WARM OVEN FOR A FEW MINUTES.

George's Venison Chili

Serves: several
Prep Time: 5 hours

BEST AFTER 24 HOURS!

2 lbs. venison stew meat
¼ cup olive oil
1 lg. bell pepper, chopped
1 lg. sweet onion, chopped
1 whole garlic clove, diced
2 30-oz. cans Caliente Style kidney beans
1 30-oz. can kidney beans
1 30-oz. can stewed tomatoes
1 8-oz. can tomato paste
3-4 stalks celery, chopped (optional)
3-4 whole jalapeno peppers
2 T. brown sugar
1 12-oz. bottle chili sauce
chili powder
cayenne pepper

Brown meat in olive oil, drain. Chop bell pepper, onion and garlic. Brown lightly. Place beans, tomatoes, tomato paste, bell pepper, garlic, celery, onion, jalapenos, brown sugar, venison and chili sauce in a 6-quart or larger crock pot or covered pot and simmer for several hours. Add chili powder and cayenne pepper to taste. Stir occasionally. Chili is ready after about 4 hours. Any meat may be substituted for the venison, the leaner the better.

George Swartzfager
Brandon, Florida

IF YOU RUN OUT OF BAKING POWDER—1 TEASPOON OF BAKING POWDER EQUALS ¼ TEASPOON BAKING SODA PLUS ½ TEASPOON CREAM OF TARTAR.

Party Pot Chili

Serves: 6-10
Prep Time: 30 minutes

2 **lbs. ground venison**
½ **lb. bacon, chopped**
1 **T. chili powder**
¼ **cup onions, chopped**
3 **cans chili beans with sauce**
2 **15-oz. cans of tomato sauce**
¼-½ **lb. cheddar cheese, shredded**

Fry ground meat, bacon, chili powder and onions until lightly brown. Mix all ingredients into pot over medium heat for about 15 minutes.

Thomas Baumgardner
Wakarusa, Kansas

Spicy Venison Chili

Serves: 4
Prep Time: 6 hours

1½ **lbs. ground venison**
1 **onion, chopped**
½ **bell pepper, chopped**
1 **quart stewed tomatoes**
1 **8-oz. can tomato sauce**
2 **16-oz. cans chili beans (drained)**
3-4 **jalapeno peppers, chopped**
½ **tsp. chili powder** ←
1 **cup celery, chopped**

FOR HOT CHILI, INCREASE CHILI POWDER TO 1½ TEASPOONS!

Brown venison, onion and bell pepper. Drain. Mix with tomatoes, tomato sauce and chili beans in crock pot. Cook for 6 hours on medium heat. Add jalapeno pepper chunks, chili powder and celery. Serve with cheddar cheese and crackers.

M. L. Lidtke
Windom, Minnesota

Chili Verde

Serves: several
Prep Time: 2 hours

> 2½ **lbs. of venison, cubed**
> 1 **T. bacon fat or vegetable oil**
> 1 **lg. onion, sliced**
> 1 **cup water**
> 2 **garlic cloves, minced**
> 12 **oz. green chiles, diced**
> 1 **med. can of peeled tomatoes, chopped**
> 2 **tsp. salt, or to taste**
> ½ **tsp. ground cumin**
> 1½ **T. flour**
> 4 **T. water**

Place fat or oil in a 5 quart saucepan and brown meat with the onion. Drain off the fat and stir in 1 cup of water and then add the rest of the ingredients except the flour. Let simmer for at least 1½ hours, stirring often to prevent it from sticking or burning.

Blend the flour with 4 tablespoons water and stir the mixture into the pot. Cook 10 minutes more until thickened. Serve with tortillas to help scoop up the sauce.

This also makes into an excellent side dish with eggs for breakfast or in an omelette.

Gene Leone
Walnut Creek, California

A QUICK CLEANUP—IF TEA IS SPILLED ON A TABLECLOTH, IT WILL WASH OUT IF SPRINKLED WITH SUGAR IMMEDIATELY.

Deer And Beer Chili

Serves: several
Prep Time: 3½ hours

4 lb. venison roast, cubed
3 lbs. mild sausage
4 med. onions
1 garlic clove
2 green chiles
2 T. oil
1 beef bouillon cube
2 T. cumin
½ tsp. dry mustard
pinch of oregano
2 12-oz. cans tomato sauce
1 12-oz. can whole tomatoes
1 oz. vodka or tequila
2 12-oz. cans beer

Chop onions, garlic and chiles fine. Brown deer and sausage in small amount of oil. Add rest of ingredients. Simmer, covered for 2½ hours, stirring occasionally. Simmer another 30 minutes without stirring. Canned beans can be an option.

Rick Cooper
Columbus, Indiana

HANDLING SOFT DOUGH—SOFT DOUGHS PRODUCE THE LIGHTEST, TENDER-CRUMBED BREAD AND ROLLS. TO MAKE THE DOUGH EASIER TO HANDLE, RUB A LITTLE SHORTENING ON YOUR FINGERS.

Sweet And Sour Venison Meatballs

Serves: varies
Prep Time: 1½ hours

GOES GREAT WITH NOODLES!

   5 lbs. ground venison
   1 lb. ground chuck
   1 onion, minced
   1 cup Italian style bread crumbs
   corn oil
   1 32-oz. bottle catsup
   1 12-oz. jar grape jelly

In large bowl, mix venison with ground chuck. Add minced onion and mix in enough bread crumbs to keep meat together and form meatballs. Cook in oil until done. In a separate pot, mix catsup and grape jelly. Heat until all of jelly is melted. Put meatballs in a roaster or crock pot and cover with sauce. Cook 1 hour at 350 degrees.

Andy Tirch
Dale City, Virginia

Easy Venison Porcupines

Serves: several
Prep Time: 6 hours

   1½ lbs. ground venison
   1 cup rice, uncooked
   garlic to taste
   1 sm. onion, diced
   ½ cup mushrooms, chopped
   2 cans tomato soup

Combine all the ingredients except soup and form into meatballs. Place in crockpot and add two cans tomato soup but only one can of water. Cover and cook on low about six hours.

Tom Squier
Aberdeen, North Carolina

Venison-Bacon Hors D'oeuvres

Serves: 10-12
Prep Time: 2 hours

 1½ **lbs. venison**
  2 **lbs. smoked bacon**
  1 **med. onion, chopped**
  ½ **cup crackers**
  1 **egg**
  ¼ **tsp. black pepper**
  1 **T. Worcestershire sauce**
  2 **T. butter**
  1 **box toothpicks**

Grind venison with ½ lb. bacon (twice). Chop onion fine.
Combine in large bowl. Crush crackers and add to mixture.
Add egg and black pepper. Mix well. Form into 1-inch round
meatballs. Fry in butter and Worcestershire sauce until brown.
Cook remainder of bacon until half done. Wrap meatballs with
bacon and skewer with toothpicks. Bake for 15 minutes at 350
degrees. Serve hot. Makes about 50.

William Czarnecki
Bristol, Connecticut

BEATING EGGS—EGGS GIVE BETTER VOLUME IF REMOVED FROM THE REFRIGERATOR LONG ENOUGH IN ADVANCE TO WARM TO ROOM TEMPERATURE BEFORE BEATING. IF WHITES AND YOLKS ARE TO BE BEATEN SEPARATELY, SEPARATE THE EGGS AS SOON AS THEY COME FROM THE REFRIGERATOR. THEY SEPARATE MORE EASILY WHEN CHILLED.

Swedish Venison Meatballs

Serves: 6-8
Prep Time: 2 hours

- **1 lb. ground venison**
- **1 lb. sausage**
- **1 tsp. salt**
- **½ tsp pepper**
- **1 onion, chopped fine**
- **½ tsp. seasoned salt**
- **2 eggs**
- **1 cup bread crumbs**
- **1 cup milk**
- **2 T. butter**
- **3 T. all-purpose flour**
- **2 cans beef gravy**
- **½ cup barbecue sauce**
- **1 cup water**
- **1 T. Worcestershire sauce**
- **1 T. soy sauce**
- **1 6-8 oz. carton sour cream**
- **¼ cup sherry (optional)**

Combine venison, sausage, salt, pepper, onions, seasoned salt, eggs, bread crumbs and milk. Form mixture into small balls. Melt butter in pan and fry balls until slightly brown. Remove from pan and pour off some fat. Add flour to pan and cook for 4 minutes. Continue stirring. Add rest of ingredients (except sherry) and keep stirring until a thick gravy is formed. Return meatballs to pan and simmer until fully cooked or put in crock pot. Add sherry towards last ½ hour before serving.

Irene Stocksdale
Dale City, Virginia

SOFTENING MARSHMALLOWS—TO SOFTEN HARD MARSHMALLOWS, PUT THEM IN A PLASTIC BAG AND DIP INTO HOT WATER.

Venison Italian Meatballs

Serves: 5
Prep Time: 1½ hours

3 lbs. ground venison
2 eggs
½ cup bread crumbs
1 onion
2 tsp. garlic powder
1 T. Worcestershire
1 tsp. Italian seasoning
2 T. butter
1 cup water
1 can pizza sauce
1 cup pizza cheese

Mix meat, eggs, bread crumbs and seasonings. Make into small balls. Brown in pan with butter. Add 1 cup water to pot and then add meatballs. Add pizza sauce and top with pizza cheese. Bake in oven for 1 hour at 300 degrees.

John Davies
Hanover, Maryland

NO CRY ONIONS—IF PEELING ONIONS MAKES YOUR EYES WATER, REFRIGERATE THE ONIONS UNTIL YOU'RE READY TO USE THEM. A COLD ONION WON'T MAKE YOUR EYES TEAR AS READILY AS ONE AT ROOM TEMPERATURE.

Swedish Meatballs

Serves: 10
Prep Time: 1 hour

- 3 lbs. venison
- 1 lb. pork sausage
- 1 tsp. salt
- 1 tsp. black pepper
- ½ tsp. cloves
- 1 tsp. nutmeg
- ½ tsp. allspice
- 4 T. brown sugar
- 2 cups chopped onions
- 4 cups bread crumbs
- 4 eggs
- 1 can cream of mushroom soup
- 1 can water

Mix all ingredients except mushroom soup and water together and form meatballs. Brown in frying pan and place meatballs in casserole dish. Add 1 can of mushroom soup and dilute with one soup can of water. Bake 45 minutes at 350 degrees.

Fred Roe
Morley, Michigan

TO REDUCE SOOT—TO KEEP A FIREPLACE CLEAN, THROW SALT ON THE LOGS OCCASIONALLY. SOOT WILL BE REDUCED BY ALMOST TWO-THIRDS.

Meatballs, A La Ozzie

Serves: 8
Prep Time: 30 minutes

> **2 lbs. ground venison**
> **½ cup oatmeal, uncooked**
> **1 egg**
> **1 T. dried onion flakes**
> **½ tsp. nutmeg**
> **dash Worcestershire sauce**
> **salt and pepper to taste**
> **3 T. cooking oil**
> **4 T. flour**
> **½ cup beer**
> **dash nutmeg**
> **4 cups cooked rice**

To form meatballs, combine first seven ingredients and mix well. Shape into balls and brown in oil. Remove meatballs from pan and make gravy by adding flour to drippings. Stir until smooth, then add beer and nutmeg. Stir meatballs into gravy. Serve over rice.

George Osborne
Jacksonville, Florida

TO CHECK IF EGG IS FRESH—IF YOU WANT TO MAKE SURE THAT AN EGG IS FRESH, PLACE IT IN A BOWL OF COLD WATER. IF IT SINKS, IT'S FRESH. IF IT'S FAIRLY FRESH, IT'LL BOB UP ON ONE END. IF IT'S STALE, IT'LL FLOAT.

Venison Meat Loaf

Serves: 4-6
Prep Time: 1 hour

   1½ **lbs. ground venison**
   ½ **lbs. ground pork**
   2 **eggs, beaten**
   1 **sm. onion, chopped**
   ½ **tsp. pepper**
   1 **tsp. salt**
   ¼ **cup brown sugar**
   ¼ **cup catsup**
   ½ **cup oatmeal**
   ½ **cup milk**
   2 **T. brown sugar**
   2 **T. catsup**

Mix all except last two ingredients in medium size bowl. Put in loaf pan. Combine brown sugar and catsup and spread over top of meat loaf. Bake at 350 degrees for 1 hour.

Wayne Umlor
Conklin, Michigan

PREVENT SCORCHING—TO PREVENT MILK FROM SCORCHING, RINSE THE SAUCEPAN IN COLD WATER AND DON'T DRY IT BEFORE ADDING THE MILK. THEN HEAT THE MILK OVER A LOW FIRE.

Berky's Venison Muffins

Serves: 6
Prep Time: 1 hour

- **1 lb. ground venison**
- **½ lb. ground pork**
- **2 cups soft bread crumbs**
- **1 cup milk**
- **1 egg, beaten**
- **1 tsp. Worcestershire sauce**
- **2 tsp. salt**
- **1 tsp. Accent**
- **½ tsp. thyme**
- **1 tsp. onion powder**
- **½ tsp. pepper**
- **1 tsp. garlic powder**
- **⅓ cup brown sugar**
- **⅓ cup catsup**

Grease muffin pan. Combine and mix above ingredients except brown sugar and catsup. Divide mixture into 12 equal portions and pack mixture lightly into wells. Bake at 350 degrees for about 40 minutes. Meanwhile, blend together and set aside cup brown sugar and catsup. After 20 minutes of baking time, spoon about 2 teaspoons catsup mixture on top of each venison muffin and continue baking. Unmold and serve hot.

Bill Berkant
Wilkes Barre, Pennsylvania

EGG CLEANUP—THE BEST WAY TO CLEAN UP A RAW EGG THAT'S BEEN DROPPED IS TO POUR SOME SALT OVER IT. LET IT STAND FOR A FEW MINUTES UNTIL THE EGG TAKES ON A POWDER FORM AND THEN SWEEP IT UP.

Crispy Venison Meat Loaves

Serves: 8
Prep Time: 30 minutes

> 1½ **lbs. ground venison**
> ¾ **cup crushed whole wheat flakes**
> 2 **eggs, beaten**
> ½ **cup onion, minced**
> 2 **T. parsley, minced**
> ½ **tsp. thyme**
> 1½ **cups whole wheat flakes, uncrushed**

Mix all ingredients except uncrushed flakes. Shape into 8
loaves about 3½ inches long. Roll in uncrushed flakes. Place in
a greased shallow pan; bake 30 minutes at 350 degrees.
Garnish with parsley and onion rings.

Wyatt Coughlan
Acton, Massachusetts

Mike's Venison Kabobs

Serves: 2-4
Prep Time: 1½ hours

> 1 **venison roast, cut in cubes**
> 4 **eggs**
> 1 **can cracker meal or bread crumbs**
> **oil**

Skewer venison cubes. Beat eggs in bowl. Pour cracker meal
or bread crumbs on 10-inch plate. Dunk meat kabobs in egg
batter and then roll in cracker meal or crumbs. Brown meat in
oil and then put on baking pan. Bake in oven at 300 degrees for
approximately 1 hour.

Michael Smalley, Sr.
Inman, South Carolina

Meat And Potato Loaf

Serves: 4-6
Prep Time: 1 hour

1 lb. browned ground venison, drained
4 cups potatoes, peeled and sliced
1 T. onion, chopped
2 tsp. salt
pepper
¾ cup canned milk
½ cup oats
¼ cup catsup
5 T. onion, chopped

Mix potatoes, 1 tablespoon onion, 1 teaspoon salt and dash of
pepper together and place in a 2 to 3 quart casserole. Then
mix rest of ingredients together and spread this mixture over
potatoes. Bake at 350 degrees, covered, 30 to 45 minutes or
until potatoes are tender.

Bobby Wright
Highland, Indiana

EASIER CHEESE GRATING—BEFORE GRATING CHEESE, PUT IT IN
THE FREEZER FOR ABOUT 40 MINUTES. THIS WILL MAKE IT EASIER TO
GRATE SINCE IT WON'T BE AS STICKY.

Venison Sausage

Serves: varies
Prep Time: 15 minutes

30 lbs. ground venison
12 lbs. ground pork
1 cup canning salt
¾ cup pepper
1 T. cloves
1 T. allspice
2 oz. nutmeg
½ cup coriander
2 tsp. garlic powder
1 cup Tender Quick
5-6 cups water

Mix meat and spices together. Add 5 to 6 cups water. Can be used for patties or cased for ring sausage.

Gordon Zurn
Waubun, Minnesota

TO FLOUR PANS—SPRINKLE EACH GREASED PAN WITH A LITTLE FLOUR; SHAKE PAN TO COAT IT EVENLY. REMOVE EXCESS FLOUR BY GENTLY KNOCKING INVERTED PAN ON WORK SURFACE.

Stuffed Venison Sausage

Serves: many
Prep Time: 2 hours

- **50 lbs. ground venison**
- **15 lbs. ground unseasoned pork**
- **¾ cup salt**
- **4 oz. bottle liquid smoke, to taste**
- **1 T. garlic salt**
- **1 T. onion salt**
- **1 8-oz. bag All American Sausage Seasoning**
- **1 T. nutmeg**
- **½ cup coarsely ground pepper**
- **½ cup crushed red pepper**
- **¼ cup Worcestershire sauce**
- **2 T. coriander**
- **2 T. caraway seeds**

Mix all ingredients and stuff in pork casings. Wrap and freeze. To serve, bake at 350 degrees for 1 hour. Serve alone or in barbecue sauce or cheese sauce.

Gordon Rasmussen
Colby, Kansas

PEEL AN EGG—IF YOU WANT A HARD-BOILED EGG TO PEEL MORE EASILY, BEGIN PEELING IT FROM THE FATTER END. THIS WILL RELEASE THE AIR POCKET AND THE SHELL WILL SLIP OFF QUICKLY.

Summer Sausage

Serves: several
Prep Time: 26 hours

> **3 lbs. ground venison**
> **1 tsp. liquid smoke**
> **2 tsp. mustard seed**
> **⅛ tsp. coarse ground pepper**
> **¼ tsp. garlic powder**
> **½ tsp. onion powder**
> **1 cup water**
> **3 T. curing salt**

GROUND ELK OR MOOSE IS GOOD, TOO!

Combine all ingredients well. Roll into three rolls. Wrap each in foil. *Shiny side in.* Refrigerate for 24 hours.

Poke holes in bottom of foil. Place in broiler pan. Bake at 325 degrees for 1½ hours. Will look reddish when done.

William Ortez
Copperas Cove, Texas

Deer Bologna

Serves: several
Prep Time: 24-48 hours

> **15 lbs. ground venison**
> **2 T. plus ⅛ tsp. black pepper**
> **¼ lb. brown sugar**
> **1³⁄₁₆ tsp. mace**
> **1³⁄₁₆ tsp. dry mustard**
> **pinch of garlic salt**
> **4 tsp. whole ground coriander**
> **1 cup plus 3½ tsp. Tender Quick**

Mix spices. Add meat and mix. Let stand for 24 to 48 hours. Then pack into sacks. Bake on cookie sheet in oven at 200 degrees for 3 to 4 hours. Turn at 2 hours.

Chris Fogle
Mathias, West Virginia

Denny's Deer Salami

Serves: several
Prep Time: overnight plus 4 hours

> **4 lbs. ground venison**
> **¼ cup Morton's Tender Quick salt**
> **2 T. liquid smoke**
> **2 tsp. black pepper**
> **2 tsp. garlic powder**
> **peppercorns**
> **honey (optional)**

Mix venison and Tender Quick Salt. Refrigerate overnight. Next day add the rest of the ingredients. Mix with hands. Divide meat into 2 rolls—it will be dry at first. Place in broiler rack and bake 4 hours at 225 degrees, turning every ½ hour. Thin coat of honey may be spread on meat before cooking, if desired. Let cool and slice thin. Serve alone or with cheese and crackers.

Dennis Cobaugh
Summerhill, Pennsylvania

JAMS, JARS AND JELLIES—WHEN FILLING JARS WITH JAMS AND JELLIES, USE A REGULAR FUNNEL LIKE YOU WOULD USE TO FILL BOTTLES. THIS WORKS LIKE A CHARM, AND YOU'LL HAVE NO STICKY RIMS. WHEN SEALING THE JARS WITH HOT PARAFFIN USE A SMALL GRAVY LADLE TO DIP UP THE MELTED PARAFFIN AND POUR IT OVER THE JAMS AND JELLIES TO SEAL THEM. THERE WILL BE NO DRIPS ON THE SIDE OF THE JARS TO CLEAN OFF.

Venison Salami

Serves: several
Prep Time: 4 days plus 6 hours

  2½ **lbs. venison**
   ½ **lb. ground beef fat** ← *BEEF FAT ADDS MOISTURE!*
  2½ **T. Morton's Tender Quick**
   ½ **tsp. Morton's Hickory Sugar Cure**
   1 **tsp. course ground pepper**
   1 **tsp. garlic powder**
  1¼ **tsp. mustard seed**
   ½ **tsp. liquid smoke**
   2 **T. brown sugar**

Mix venison and ground beef fat together. In a large bowl, mix meat and all ingredients together by hand. Cover and refrigerate for 3 days. Each day remove and knead meat thoroughly. On 4th day, roll meat in 1½-inch to 2-inch rolls, 6 inches long. Use meat rack on cookie sheet to catch grease drippings and cook 6 hours at 150 degrees, turning rolls each hour. Let cool and slice and serve. They can be frozen for future use.

Neil Thompson
Upper Marlboro, Maryland

A CANNING SHORTCUT—A SHORTCUT IN PREPARING TOMATOES FOR CANNING IS TO PUT THE COOKED, QUARTERED TOMATOES IN THE BLENDER FOR A FEW SECONDS BEFORE RUNNING THEM THROUGH A COLANDER. THIS SAVES A LOT OF TIME AND THE JUICE TURNS OUT MUCH THICKER.

Venison Thuringer

Serves: several
Prep Time: 80 hours

OTHER GAME MEAT GOOD, TOO!

- **5 lbs. ground venison**
- **5 tsp. Morton's Tender Quick Salt**
- **2½ tsp. mustard seed**
- **3½ tsp. garlic salt**
- **3 tsp. liquid smoke**
- **¼ tsp. cayenne**
- **3 tsp. peppercorns**

Mix all ingredients together and refrigerate for 24 hours.

Day 2: Again, mix all ingredients well and refrigerate for another 24 hours.

Day 3: Repeat day 2.

Day 4: Divide mixture into 3 equal rolls (like salami) and place in broiler pan. Bake in oven at 150 degrees for 8 hours, turning every 2 hours. Cool and refrigerate. Serve sliced like salami.

James Merwin
Manteca, California

Venison Sausage Balls

Serves: several
Prep Time: 45 minutes

- **1 lb. hot or mild venison sausage**
- **1 lb. sharp cheese, grated**
- **3 cups Bisquick mix**
- **2 T. water**

Fry and crumble sausage. Mix all ingredients together in a bowl. Roll into balls with hands. Bake at 350 degrees for 30 minutes or until brown.

Lowell Tinsley
Hamilton, Ohio

Venison Soup

Serves: 6-8
Prep Time: 8½ hours

1 lg. venison shank bone, cut into 3 pieces
2 lbs. venison shank meat
2 beef bouillon cubes
2 bay leaves
½ tsp. savory
1 T. peppercorns
1 onion slice
several celery leaves
2 lbs. canned tomatoes
1 med. onion, diced
2 celery ribs, thinly sliced
3 carrots, sliced
3 med. potatoes, diced
¼ cup chopped parsley
salt to taste

Place the shank bone and meat in large pot with enough water to cover the bone and meat. Add bouillon, bay leaves, savory, peppercorns, onion slice and celery leaves. Place over high heat and bring to a boil. Cover and simmer for at least 8 hours. Remove meat and bone from the broth. Strain broth to remove bay leaves and vegetables. If there is any fat on top, skim it off. Pour broth back into large pot and add tomatoes, diced onion and sliced celery. Cook for 15 minutes. Add carrots and let cook 10 more minutes. Add potatoes and parsley and let cook 10 more minutes. Add salt to taste.

Leroy Hegge
Erlanger, Kentucky

DE-SALT SOUP—IF SOUP IS TOO SALTY, SLICE A RAW POTATO INTO SOUP AND ALLOW TO BOIL FOR A SHORT TIME. REMOVE POTATO.

Venison Pâte

Serves: varies
Prep Time: 24½ hours

½ **lb. liver, sliced**
½ **lb. heart, sliced** ⟵ DUCK, PHEASANT, GOOSE LIVERS AND HEARTS MAY ALSO BE USED!
4 **T. butter**
3 **hard cooked eggs**
3 **3-oz. pkgs. cream cheese, softened**
1 **tsp. salt**
¼ **tsp. ground fresh pepper**
4 **T. cognac (brandy)**
3 **truffles, coarsely chopped (mushrooms can be used)**

Melt butter in sauce pan. Add sliced liver and heart. Cook, stirring frequently until tender, 8 to 10 minutes. Work eggs, liver and heart through a food grinder, blender or food processor. Work cream cheese until soft, then combine with the ground meat mixture. Make this as smooth as possible. Stir in salt, pepper, cognac and truffles. If too thick, thin with consommé. Refrigerate. This needs 24 hours to set up. Makes about 20 ounces.

H. F. Henriques
Orr, Minnesota

WARMING DINNER ROLLS—TO WARM DINNER ROLLS WHEN YOUR OVEN IS IN USE, PUT THEM IN YOUR SLOW COOKER ON LOW HEAT FOR ABOUT 30 TO 40 MINUTES. THEY'LL COME OUT WARM AND DELICIOUS.

Venison Heart Teriyaki

Serves: 2-4
Prep Time: ½ hour

- **1 venison heart**
- **2 T. butter**
- **4 T. teriyaki or soy sauce**
- **2 T. olive or vegetable oil**
- **1 med. onion, diced**
- **salt and pepper**

DON'T OVERCOOK VENISON HEART!

Slice heart into ½-inch slices. In a frying pan, heat butter, soy sauce and olive oil on medium heat. Add diced onions and cook until tender. Place slices of heart in pan and cook 2 minutes on each side. Don't overcook, as heart will become tough and dry. Salt and pepper to taste. Serve with a favorite side dish.

Sylvain Turcotte
Newcomb, New York

A SIMPLE DOUBLE BOILER—A LARGE SOUP LADLE CAN SERVE AS A DOUBLE BOILER WHEN PLACED IN A SMALL PAN OF BOILING WATER. USE IT TO MELT CHOCOLATE, BUTTER OR HEAT BABY FOOD.

Marinated Venison Heart

Serves: 3-4
Prep Time: overnight plus 2 hours

- 1 **venison heart**
- 1 **med. red or white onion, sliced thin**
- 1½ **cups red wine vinegar**
- ⅓ **cup water**
- ¼ **tsp. salt**
- 8-10 **peppercorns**
- 2 **bay leaves**
- 2 **garlic cloves**

Rinse and clean heart. Soak overnight in cold salted water (approximately 1 cup salt to 1 quart water). To prepare: Add 1 cup of salt to 1 quart of fresh cold water. Simmer heart in salted water for 45 to 60 minutes. Cool and trim off fat. Cut heart in half, peel off outer membrane and slice thin. Alternate layers of onion and heart. Add the rest of the combined ingredients and refrigerate. Serve on crackers or wheat toast.

Alfred Sabino
Ringwood, New Jersey

A MORE ACCURATE MEASURE—WHEN MEASURING SHORTENING FOR A CAKE, BREAK THE EGG IN THE CUP FIRST AND POUR IT OUT. THE SHORTENING WILL NOT STICK TO THE CUP.

Pickled Venison Heart

Serves: 2
Prep Time: 1-2 hours

    1 venison heart
    ½ tsp. brown sugar
    3 sm. white onions
    ⅓ quart cold water
    ½ tsp. salt
    ½ tsp. black pepper
       white cider vinegar

Set aside 1 quart jar. Boil heart in kettle filled with enough
water to cover heart. When water starts to boil add brown
sugar and boil until cooked through, 30 to 45 minutes. Drain
heart and cool in refrigerator. Dice heart into chunks, slice
onions in thin slices. Mix onions and meat and place in quart
jar. Add ⅓ quart cold water. Put in salt and pepper. Finish
filling jar with white cider vinegar. Place cover on jar, shake
twice and place in refrigerator. Leave two to three days and
then enjoy. Water and vinegar mix can be changed to suit your
own taste.

Carroll Curtis
Massona, New York

SHUCKING WALNUTS—TO GET WALNUT MEATS OUT OF THEIR
SHELLS WHOLE, SOAK THE NUTS OVERNIGHT IN SALTWATER BEFORE YOU
CRACK THEM.

Venison Sauce

Serves: 4
Prep Time: 3-4 hours

2 lbs. ground venison
1 lb. ground beef or sausage
1 T. oil
1 cup onions, chopped
1 tsp. seasoned salt
1 tsp. salt
1 tsp. pepper
1 cup hickory sauce
2 T. soy sauce
2 T. Worcestershire sauce
4 6-oz. cans tomato sauce
4 6-oz. cans tomato paste
2 cups water
4 4-oz. cans sliced mushrooms
2 14-oz. cans peeled tomatoes

TRY A LITTLE HOT SAUCE!

Brown meat in oil for 30 minutes, then add onions until brown. Continue stirring. Add seasoned salt, salt, pepper, hickory sauce, soy sauce and Worcestershire sauce. Continue to stir and let simmer for another 30 minutes. Add tomato sauce and paste, mixing sauce and paste together with 2 cups of water before adding. Add mushrooms and tomatoes.

After all ingredients are combined together, let simmer again for 1 to 2 hours. Continue to stir. Serve over noodles or let cool to put in jars for later.

Irene Stocksdale
Dale City, Virginia

SPICE UP LEFTOVERS—THROW TOMATO JUICE AND CHILI POWDER IN WITH LEFTOVER BEANS OR LENTILS FOR A QUICK, SPICY SOUP.

Venison Pizza

Serves: 6-8
Prep Time: 2 hours

1 lb. ground venison
6 cups unbleached flour
1½ cups buttermilk
4 T. butter or margarine
4 T. honey
½ tsp. salt
1 pkg. yeast
¼ cup warm water
3 cups grated cheese
1 sm. onion, chopped
chives (optional)
2 cans pizza sauce
oregano
garlic powder
pepper
thyme

First, measure flour into large bowl. In a separate container combine buttermilk, butter, honey and salt. Heat the buttermilk mixture to lukewarm. Dissolve yeast in warm water. Add yeast and milk mixture to flour and combine to make a firm dough. Turn dough out and knead for about 5 minutes, or until it is smooth and elastic. Put the dough in a greased bowl, cover and let rise until double in bulk, about 1 hour. While dough is rising, prepare the toppings. Grate plenty of cheese.

Chop some onions and some wild chives if you have some handy. Fry venison, crumbling it as you fry. When dough has risen, punch it down, divide it in half, and roll out the two parts to fit your baking sheets. The dough should be about ¼-inch thick. Let the rolled out dough rise for about 15 minutes. Spread a generous amount of pizza sauce on the dough. Sprinkle on plenty of oregano, garlic powder, pepper and a little thyme. Top with grated cheese and the crumbled venison. Bake at 350 degrees for 20 to 30 minutes.

Mary Smith
Lewiston, Minnesota

North Country Spread

Serves: several
Prep Time: 30 minutes

LEFTOVER ROAST WORKS WELL!

1 lb. cooked venison roast
1 cup undrained red and green pepper relish
⅓ cup onion, chopped
⅓ cup pickles, diced
½ cup celery, diced
2 T. mustard
½ cup mayonnaise

Grind cooked roast or chop in processor or blender. Combine pepper relish, onions, pickle and celery and add to ground meat. Stir mustard into mayonnaise to make a spreadable consistency. May be used for sandwiches or crackers.

Terry Quayle
Ishpeming, Michigan

Buck's Venison Cheese Dip

Serves: several
Prep Time: 1 hour

1 lb. ground venison
1 log Velveeta cheese
2 sm. cans jalapeno peppers   *CAN BE*
   red hot sauce   *HOT OR MILD!*
1 bag tortilla chips

Spray crockpot with Pam and turn it on high. Cube cheese, add to crockpot and cover. This will melt quicker. Brown meat in fry pan. Drain off grease. When cheese is melted, add meat and peppers to crockpot. Mix well. Reduce heat. If needed, add a few drops of red hot sauce to taste. Leave covered and on low until ready to serve with your favorite tortilla chips.

C.R. Raphael
Columbus, Ohio

Alfred's Oriental Venison Jerky

Serves: several
Prep Time: 24 hours

  4 lb. venison roast
  ¼ cup salt
  ¼ cup brown sugar
  2 cups water
  1 cup apple cider/or cider vinegar
  ½ cup soy sauce
  2 oz. bourbon or brandy
  ½ tsp. onion powder
  ½ tsp. garlic powder
  1 tsp. grated ginger
  1 tsp. grated orange peel
  6 white cloves (optional)

Trim fat from meat and cut into ¼- to ½-inch thick slices. Place meat into the marinade made by combining the above ingredients in a glass or ceramic bowl. Marinate at least 8 hours in a cool place. Remove to a rack and allow to air dry until they become glazed. Do not rinse. Smoke for 12 to 16 hours depending on degree of desired dryness. Use approximately 3 panfuls of hickory or cherry wood chips to add flavor.

Alfred Sabino
Ringwood, New Jersey

REFRIGERATE JERKY—ALTHOUGH JERKY WILL NOT SPOIL AT ROOM TEMPERATURE, IT IS ADVISABLE TO REFRIGERATE IT IF IT IS TO BE STORED FOR A LONG PERIOD OF TIME.

Alfred's Spicy Venison Jerky

Serves: several
Prep Time: 24 hours

   4 lb. venison roast
   ⅓ cup brown sugar
   ¼ cup salt
   2 cups soy sauce
   1 cup water
   1 cup red wine
   ½ tsp. onion powder
   ½ tsp. pepper
   ½ tsp. garlic powder
   ½ tsp. Tabasco sauce

Trim fat from meat and cut into ¼- to ½-inch thick slices. Place meat into the marinade made by combining the above ingredients in a glass or ceramic bowl. Marinate at least 8 hours in a cool place. Remove to a rack and allow to air dry until they become glazed. Do not rinse. Smoke for 12 to 16 hours depending on degree of desired dryness. Use approximately 3 panfuls of hickory or cherry wood chips to add flavor.

Alfred Sabino
Ringwood, New Jersey

MARBLES IN YOUR POT—PUT MARBLES IN THE WATER IN THE BOTTOM OF A DOUBLE BOILER. WHEN THE WATER BOILS DOWN, THE MARBLES WILL MAKE ENOUGH RACKET TO CALL YOU EVEN IF YOU'RE OUTSIDE SPLITTIN' WOOD.

Deer Jerky

Serves: varies
Prep Time: 28 hours

3-4 lbs. venison
4 T. onion powder
1⅓ tsp. black pepper
1⅓ tsp. garlic powder
2 pinches salt
½ tsp. Italian seasoning
1 cup Worcestershire sauce
1 cup soy sauce
1 tsp. Texas Pete

Cut meat into ¼-inch strips or less, cutting with the grain.
Combine rest of ingredients. Place meat in pan or dish and
pour marinade over meat. Let stand 24 hours in refrigerator.
Remove from refrigerator and place foil in bottom of oven to
catch drippings. Insert toothpicks through one end of strip of
meat and hang from oven rack. Rack should be at highest
setting. Bake at 150 degrees for 4 hours or until dried to taste.

James Glass, Jr.
Mineral, Virginia

SIMPLE PARAFFIN REMOVERS—SAVE THE METAL PULL TABS
FROM POP CANS TO USE WHEN MAKING JAMS OR JELLIES. PLACE A TAB
IN THE LIQUID PARAFFIN JUST BEFORE IT HARDENS. THIS MAKES AN
EXCELLENT PARAFFIN REMOVER.

Venison Jerky

Serves: several
Prep Time: 10 hours

    5 lbs. venison, boned
    3 tsp. Tender Quick
    2 tsp. black pepper
    1 tsp. liquid smoke
    ½ cup spicy brown mustard
    ½ cup light corn syrup
    ½ tsp. garlic salt or powder
    ½ tsp. onion salt or powder
    2 pinches tarragon
    1 tsp. Worcestershire sauce

Cut venison into fairly thick slices. Mix remaining ingredients. Lay strips of venison on broiler pans. Coat with sauce, salt and pepper to taste. Flip, coat with sauce, pepper and salt again to taste. Bake approximately 6 hours at 150 degrees. Flip and continue to bake another 4 hours. Allow to cool, then place in covered containers or plastic bags. Flavor will "peak" in a day or two.

Kyle Geno
Dryden, Michigan

PROTECT YOUR ASPARAGUS—ALWAYS OPEN A CAN OF ASPARAGUS FROM THE BOTTOM. THE STALKS WILL SLIP OUT WITHOUT INJURING THE FRAGILE TOPS.

Sugar Cured Venison Jerky

Serves: several
Prep Time: overnight plus 8 hours

>   **5 lbs. venison roast**
> **1½ cups sugar**
>   **1 tsp. brown sugar**
> **15 tsp. salt**
>   **1 oz. liquid smoke**
>   **2 tsp. garlic**
>   **3 tsp. seasoning salt**
>   **1 tsp. black pepper**

Cut venison 1 to 2 inches wide and ¼-inch thick, 6 to 10 inches long. Put in large mixing bowl and add sugar a little at a time. Be sure to mix well. Mix brown sugar and all other spices and mix all together. Put in refrigerator approximately 6 to 8 hours. Take out and put in oven on racks, lightly pepper. Cook at a maximum of 150 degrees until completely dry, approximately 8 hours.

John Poletti
Marietta, Oklahoma

Venison Beans

Serves: 4-6
Prep Time: 30 minutes

> **1-2 lbs. ground venison**
>   **2 cans pork and beans**
>   **1 cup mustard**
>   **1 cup catsup**
>   **1 onion, cut up**
>   **1 green pepper, cut up**

Brown venison in fry pan. Add remainder of ingredients and simmer until mixed and hot to serve.

Michael Smalley, Sr.
Inman, South Carolina

Mike's Beans

Serves: 4-6
Prep Time: 4½ hours

  2 lbs. venison
  1 lb. bacon
  1 can pork and beans
  1 can lima beans
  1 can kidney beans
  1 can navy beans
  ½ onion, cut up
  1 green pepper, cut up
  1 cup mustard
  1 cup catsup
  1 tsp. brown sugar
  1 tsp. salt
  1 tsp. pepper

Brown venison and bacon. Put all ingredients in crock pot and cook for 4 hours on high temperature setting.

Michael Smalley, Sr.
Inman, South Carolina

Canned Venison

Wash meat well and cut up in one-inch cubes, removing all fat. Pat dry and pack quart jars until full. Do not add water or salt. Secure lids and process for 90 minutes at 10 lbs. pressure. The venison will make its own juice and a layer of fat will be on top. This will keep for a long time and can be used for several dishes, such as vegetable and venison stew. Or, you can turn out the contents of a jar into a skillet and warm well. Make gravy and cook potatoes and you have a meal.

Lowell Tinsley
Hamilton, Ohio

Canned Smoke & Sour Venison Stew

Serves: 4-6
Prep Time: 1½ hours

- **1 cup venison stew meat**
- **⅓ cup lima beans**
- **⅓ cup string beans**
- **⅓ cup carrots, sliced**
- **⅓ cup celery, sliced**
- **2 T. onion, chopped**
- **½ tsp. garlic, sliced**
- **2 T. home cured venison ham**
- **1 beef bouillon cube**
- **1 cup potatoes, diced**
- **½ tsp. salt**
- **½ tsp. Worcestershire sauce**
- **⅛ cup sour wine**
- **1 T. Drake's crispy fry mix**
  warm water

Pack raw ingredients in quart jar in above order to within one inch of top, seal and process for 90 minutes at 10 lbs. pressure.

Willard Foster
Midland, Michigan

FILLING YOUR FREEZER BAGS—TO FILL FREEZER BAGS EASILY: PLACE FOOD IN A JAR, SLIP THE BAG OVER THE MOUTH OF THE JAR, AND INVERT. THE BAG IS QUICKLY FILLED WITH THE FOOD AND THE TOP IS CLEAN FOR SEALING.

Smokin' Up A Storm

Proven recipes and techniques for smoking wild game. Author Thayne Smith first smoked wild game during the Depression when he hunted squirrels for food. He has created and refined smoking recipes for more than 50 years. In this chapter, he gives you these recipes and his time-tested techniques. Thayne also provides you with info on the flavors various woods yield. Oak, he says, yields a mellow, fresh flavor that is best for steaks, wild boar, grouse and prairie chicken.

Smokin' Up A Storm

by Thayne Smith

An old college professor once noted that the first artists probably were cave men who drew pictures on rocks with charred sticks.

I've often wondered, since being kicked out of his class for asking silly questions, if the sticks were the remains of some of the first outdoor cooking endeavors? And, were the cave dwellers artists at whomping up half a javelina on a spit, or skewering a rump roast from a mastodon over a hickory-charcoal fire?

History books and old college profs tell us a lot about artists, but they don't waste much time on the fine art of outdoor cooking.

However, every culture in the world has outdoor cookery in its past. It probably started when some neolithic hunter dropped a drumstick in the fire and found it tasted better than dodo bird in the raw.

Next, he learned to roast meats over the fire, on a stick, and that tasted even better.

He learned, probably again by accident, to use fire, smoke and moisture to cook his meals slowly to a tender, flavorful, uncharred turn. No doubt it was appetizing, even without barbecue sauce, which wasn't to come along for some time.

In fact, it is still popular among adventuresome hunters to turn a roast of elk, an upland game bird or two, a duck, a goose or a hunk of javelina on a hand-crank spit positioned between two forked sticks over a hardwood fire.

The secret is in the pre-cooking preparation of the meat or fowl, and the selection of the wood for the smoking process.

It's too bad I didn't know these things 45 years ago when on a cross-country hunting trip with a bunch of rowdy friends during high school days.

Smoking wild game is practical and affordable thanks to the development of small smoker ovens for residential use, like this Coleman Cookin' Machine. They are ideal for the flavoring of venison, upland birds and waterfowl.
—Photo courtesy of The Coleman Company

We first shot a pheasant, then a jackrabbit, and decided we should have a primitive-type feast. There are few trees on the plains of Western Kansas, but we finally found an elm with two forked limbs, and fashioned a spit of sorts to cook our bounty.

Pheasant and jackrabbit cooked hurriedly over an elm fire, without salt, pepper or barbecue sauce, are no delicacy, believe me.

I recalled the adventure years later when watching "Gunsmoke," the old Dodge City show, on black-and-white television.

Marshal Matt Dillon and sidekick, Festus Haggis, were caught in a storm while on the plains chasing bandits, and had to turn to nature for a meal. Matt harvested a prairie chicken on the wing with his rifle (it was an easy shot, of course), and Festus cooked it on a spit not unlike that which we fashioned of elm.

Matt and Festus didn't say what kind of wood they were using, but they gnawed and gnashed at the prairie chicken drumsticks, remarking that it was an "old bird" but "it sure was good."

It was evident that the scriptwriters knew nothing about hunting or prairie chickens. They're not easy to take on the wing with a rifle, and everyone knows that even the gravy is tough when you cook an old one.

My first lessons in smoking meat, and wild game, came in Arkansas at the age of six, when my folks moved from the Kansas plains to escape the Dust Bowl.

The Ozark farm they purchased had three outbuildings—a barn, an outhouse and a smokehouse. The only running water was in a creek a mile away. The smokehouse was my mother's "refrigerator" and "pantry."

A small building of six by eight feet or so, it had rough-hewn side boards, hand-split oak shingles, some shelves on the side, and an earthen floor. It wasn't exactly a carpenter's showpiece, with enough cracks and holes to let the smoke billow out the sides. Large rocks were used to form a fire ring, about four feet in diameter, in the center, and wires

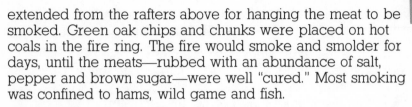

extended from the rafters above for hanging the meat to be smoked. Green oak chips and chunks were placed on hot coals in the fire ring. The fire would smoke and smolder for days, until the meats—rubbed with an abundance of salt, pepper and brown sugar—were well "cured." Most smoking was confined to hams, wild game and fish.

Rabbits and squirrels were plentiful in that part of the world. They were generally consumed (fried) shortly after being harvested or were smoked for a few days, then "canned."

With no electricity, refrigeration or ice box, there were only two ways to preserve meats—by smoking, or "canning" in a pressure cooker.

Canning, in fact, became an important factor in my life on Christmas Day, 1940. I was 11 years old, and was presented my first gun—a gleaming Remington .22 single shot—and one box of shells.

I headed for the woods on our farm, with my dog—a fine collie that was excellent at "treeing" squirrels.

A happy and proud hunter and his dog returned with 16 squirrels four hours later, but my folks weren't too impressed.

Dad, I recall, lectured me considerably while teaching me how to clean squirrels and "fire up" the smokehouse, and Mother let me know she didn't appreciate having to "can" squirrels during the holidays.

Some credit the Chinese with the invention of the smoking process to preserve foods, and the Gauls with the first bacon-curing methods.

Others acknowledge smoking processes developed by Indians in the Northwestern United States for curing fish and wild game.

The colonists of early America had no refrigeration or means of preserving meats other than salting and drying, or slow curing with cook smoke in fragrant smokehouses.

Smoke-cured meats are preserved, but not fully cooked. They take supplemental cooking, by frying, baking or roasting, before being served.

Today, cooking out of doors and smoking wild game is a favorite of many North American Hunting Club members.

Some still use the "cold smoke process" of Colonial and pioneer days for curing wild game, while others enjoy a second smoking process—called "smoke cookery"—which uses a low fire, hot smoke and sometimes moisture, to provide a complete job.

Smoke cooking popularity soared two decades ago with the development of a variety of small smoker ovens for residential use. They are ideal for the cooking and flavoring of wild game, upland birds and waterfowl.

Most prominent are the "water" smokers, using propane (or natural gas), charcoal and/or wood, or electricity as a fuel source. Made of steel, they employ a water pan between the fuel source and the meat shelves. The pan provides moisture for the game being cooked, and catches the juices as they drip from the meat.

Others, also quite prominent, can be used to cure and flavor wild game meats, but require the use of an oven or microwave to complete the cooking process.

There are many do-it-yourself smokers in use, too. Some are modeled after the outdoor smokehouses of old, while others are made of culvert pipe, hollow logs, wooden barrels, metal drums, packing boxes, frame and canvas cylinders and old refrigerator bodies.

Popular with avid hunters and outdoorsmen are elaborate backyard smokers made of brick, concrete block and stone, some identical to home building materials.

Even tiny smokers for indoor use, using wood shavings and chunks for flavor, are now available.

After all this, you would think that it is easy to smoke-cook just about anything in the "wild game" category.

Not so. To be a gourmet smoker-cook, you must first remember that wild game is different, and smoking is an art. It's nothing like cooking on a stove.

Game, of course, comes in many sizes, shapes and cuts, from nuggets to quarters. Smoke-cooking wild animals and fowl is

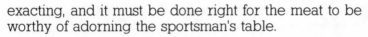

exacting, and it must be done right for the meat to be worthy of adorning the sportsman's table.

First, you must use a reliable thermometer. They're expensive, but worth it. Cheap ones will not help. Expert cooks and most smoker manufacturers recommend internal temperatures of 145 to 225 degrees Fahrenheit for wild game. Follow their advice on various types of meat, and cook them to the temperatures they recommend for tastes of rare, medium or well-done.

Remember, too, that wild game is much leaner than domesticated animal meats. This accounts for much of the popularity of the water smoker, because others remove the moisture from fat-free meat. (Moisture removal is desirable in some cooking, however, such as the making of jerky from venison cuts). The water smoker, in effect, lets the meat cook in its own juices.

Water smokers allow for wood chips or chunks to be added to the fuel source, to create a moist smoke which prevents wild meat from drying.

And, they're versatile. They become barbecue grills if the water is removed, roasters if the water and wood are eliminated or steamers if the wood is removed and the water pan filled.

Some gourmet cooks use other liquids and spices in the water pan to flavor the wild meat and make sauces or gravies of the drippings. Favorites are beer, wine, cider, fruit juices or marinades. Some add herbs and spices.

Often, when the cooking is done, there is some fine brew left in the pan. It can be spooned over the meat when served, made into a sauce or gravy, or refrigerated or frozen to use to make soup.

The pan should be lifted carefully out of the unit when cooking is completed, and the juices poured into a large measure or bowl. Let stand briefly so fat can come to the surface and be removed, and juices tasted for concentration and seasoning.

Caution should be used to make sure the pans do not cook dry. Much of the liquid will evaporate from heat during the long smoking process, so the level in the pan should be checked periodically (every four hours is sufficient).

At the same time, it's not good to fuss over the meat or constantly remove the smoker lid. This allows heat and moisture to escape and prolongs cooking time.

Another prime ingredient in smoke-cooking perfection is the selection of the wood used to provide the smoke.

Tastes and choices differ from one cook to the next, and often depend on the type and texture of game being prepared.

No doubt, every kind of wood known has been tried for smoking. Some, however, are not good.

The national favorite—and mine—is hickory, with mesquite, oak, fruit woods (cherry, apple, peach), alder, nut woods (walnut, pecan) and even grapevines being used to add new flavors.

Without a doubt, green woods are best. Any dry chunks used should be soaked in water for at least 30 minutes, and put on the charcoal or in the wood pan prior to placing the meat on the grill or rack. Chips are best for food that cooks fast, such as steaks and chops, quail or dove. Chunks are preferred with large fowl (turkey, goose, pheasant), roasts or briskets. (Some commercial "chips" appear to be little more than sawdust, but they work well.)

Here's a brief rundown on the flavors provided by the various woods:

Hickory: Strong, pungent, smoky. Best for robust food such as roasts (deer, moose, elk, caribou, pronghorn) and bear.

Mesquite: Strong, sweet, rich and woody. Best for meats that stand up to strong taste, including waterfowl, quail, dove, pheasant, grouse and venison.

Oak: Mellow and fresh. Best for meats with strong flavor, such as steaks, wild boar, grouse and prairie chicken.

Alder: Sweet and delicate. Best for thick steaks, javelina and game birds with light meat.

Fruit woods: Light and lingering. Best for small waterfowl.

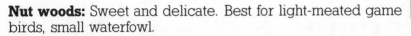

Nut woods: Sweet and delicate. Best for light-meated game birds, small waterfowl.

Grapevine: Sweet and tangy. Best for goat, antelope, quail, chukar, dove.

A word of caution. Never use wood chips or chunks which include the bark of the tree or vine, or grass, leaves or moss as a fuel source. They impart a strong, bitter taste to the meat being cooked.

I have never used birch, but understand it is a fine cooking wood. I've been tempted to try ash and hackberry, but I don't experiment often when there's green hickory at my back door.

One experience with elm, even in clumsy, boyhood fashion, was enough. Cottonwood is another prominent plains wood, but it isn't worth a twit for smoking. It's too soft.

Unusual, and a real surprise, is Osage orange—the wood of "hedgerows" which abound in some midwest states and provide excellent wildlife cover. The Coleman Company, of Wichita, Kansas, packs a bag of hedge chunks with each of its fine portable smokers.

Interesting, isn't it, that some of the wildlife we enjoy smoking is afforded protection by the woods we use in their preparation, *after both are harvested*?

If you're truly an adventurous wild game cook, be daring, experiment and try something different once in a while.

For instance, wood chips made from Jack Daniels whiskey barrels are now available. Their aroma is tantalizing, and the taste they lend to wild game meat will make a big hit with your guests, while you enjoy smokin' up a storm.

Recipes For Smoking, Cooking Wild Game

Some of the finest recipes come by accident, and those that include wild game are no exception.

Several years ago, my wife Joan and I planned to entertain several friends at our home on New Year's Eve.

She was preparing a large pot of long-favorite chili, made from scratch with lean beef, while I used a charcoal-fueled water smoker to prepare hors d'oeuvres of newly harvested quail and dove breasts, pheasant and prairie chicken.

All plans were perfect, except that I forgot to include the water pan in the smoker.

With a big pan of charcoal topped with hickory chips, the birds were a little more than "well done" when I (luckily) checked on their progress after about two hours.

The dove and quail breasts had been wrapped in bacon to help keep them moist, and were on the top shelf. They were edible when cut in chunks. The same was true of the pheasant and prairie chicken breasts. Cut in small squares, they made excellent finger food.

The legs and thighs were not burned, but were dry and somewhat stringy. I was going to toss them, but noticed Joan's chili simmering on the stove.

I removed all but the toughest of the thigh and leg meat, trimmed off the tough outer skin, cut it in tiny chunks and chucked it in the chili.

Within a few minutes, the aroma of the chili turned to a pleasing "smoke" smell, as the pheasant and prairie chicken mingled and mixed with the other ingredients.

It didn't take our guests long to ask "what's cookin" when they entered the home, and I knew by then that we had a winner.

Good smoking recipes can be hard to find. This chapter includes many of the author's favorites, and favorites from industry experts.—Photo courtesy of The Coleman Company

The chili was marvelous—rich and flavorful, with a hickory-smoke tang that proved a highlight of the evening.

Joan's chili, with a bit of smoked wild game added (we've tried several things since that first "accident," and they're all good) now tops the list of our "smoked wild game" recipes.

Joan's Chili

Serves: 10
Prep Time: 3 hours

> 3 **lbs. ground chuck or 2 lbs. chuck and 1 lb.**
> **ground venison, elk or moose**
> 1 **cup finely chopped smoked meat,**
> **preferably pheasant, quail or grouse**
> 3 **T. suet, finely chopped**
> 3 **cups water**
> 2 **cups dry red kidney or pinto beans,**
> **pre-cooked**
> 1¼ **cups canned tomatoes**
> ½ **cup chopped onion**
> 1½ **T. chili powder**
> 1 **tsp. sugar**
> 1 **tsp. salt**
> ½ **bay leaf**
> **pinch of cayenne pepper**
> **few drops of Tabasco sauce**

Fry suet until liquid. Add ground and smoked meat and brown.
Add water, beans, tomatoes and onions, then seasonings. Heat
to a boil; reduce to simmer. Cover and cook at least 2 hours.
Check and stir often. Add water as needed.

Brine And Marinades

The preparation of many smoked wild game dishes is
enhanced by seasoning and "liquid curing" with brines and
marinades. Some are basic, while others range to exotic.

Following are simple recipes for a pre-smoking brine that is
excellent for most wild game, and two recipes for
marinades—one for red meat and the other for anything.

Basic Brine

¼ cup non-iodized salt
¼ cup white sugar
1 quart water
  juice of ½ lemon (optional)

In a quart or one-half gallon plastic container or jar combine salt and sugar and mix first with ½-quart of warm water. Then combine with ½-quart of cold water, and add lemon if desired. (A little lemon juice enhances the flavor of most wild meat[]!) If not used immediately, store in refrigerator. *Keep cold.*

When you feel like experimenting, add herbs, spices and other seasonings to the mixture.

You'll find the following useful in developing your own brines and marinades:

Spices: Caraway, cayenne, celery seed, cloves, curry, ginger, mace, nutmeg, pepper, peppercorns, iodized salt, tumeric.

Herbs: Basil, bay, dill, oregano, marjoram, parsley, rosemary, sage, tarragon, thyme.

Other flavor enhancers: Garlic, lemon, lime, onion, monosodium glutamate, fruit juices (apple, pineapple, orange, cherry), seasoning salts, Worcestershire sauce, commercial sauces such as Tabasco, Kitchen Bouquet, A-1, Heinz 57 and barbecue.

Add honey, molasses, brown sugar, wine, rum, bourbon, chili sauce, soy, catsup and any berry juices you particularly like.

Brines should be mixed in glass or plastic containers only. Wooden or aluminum vessels should not be used. Brine ingredients will cause the taste of wood or metal to penetrate the liquid.

Meats should be completely covered by brines when possible, then turned occasionally. Keep them cool by storing in a refrigerator.

Rinse meat with cool water after brining and before smoking.

Marinades, like brines, vary with each gourmet cook, and the meat to be smoked.

Actually, once he or she finds a favorable basic recipe, it becomes the product of the cook's imagination.

Okie Marinade

⅓ **cup lemon juice**
2 **cups red wine**
½ **cup soy sauce**
¼ **cup vinegar**
1 **T. Worcestershire sauce**
½ **tsp. Tabasco sauce**
¼ **cup honey**
3 **tsp. brown sugar**
½ **tsp. garlic powder**
1 **T. non-iodized salt**
4 **T. pepper**

This recipe is a good one which I've developed over the years for smoking. Mix all ingredients well. Add meat to marinade and refrigerate for 6 hours or more. Remove meat, pat dry with towel (don't rinse) and place in smoker. Follow manufacturer's suggestions for smoking and cooking time, which will vary with "wet" or "dry" smoking units.

Vary it a little with the use of different spices, juices and herbs. It's great for just about any wild game you intend to smoke.

Red Meat Marinade

½ **cup soy sauce**
¼ **cup oil**
¼ **cup white wine or sherry**
1 **tsp. Worcestershire sauce**
1 **tsp. garlic powder**
big dash of fresh ground pepper

Mix ingredients well. Marinate meat for 8 to 12 hours in the refrigerator. Keep cool. Pat dry with paper towel when removed. Smoke in your favorite way. This is a quick, easy-to-make marinade that goes extremely well with any red wild meat, including venison, elk, moose, bear, antelope, horsemeat, sheep and reindeer.

Dove Special

Serves: 6-8
Prep Time: 4 hours

15-20 dove breasts
1 carrot, diced
1 two-inch square of cheddar cheese, finely
grated
1 med. white onion, chopped
1 can mushroom soup
1 carton sour cream
dash of garlic salt
dash of onion salt
2 T. flour
fresh ground pepper
4-5 ripe olives, diced
1 T. chopped pimentos
3 T. butter

First, brown dove breasts in a dry smoker, with apple or
cherry chips, for about two hours. Place in a single layer in a
large glass dish, and prepare a "gravy" of the remaining
ingredients. Mix the ingredients well, and pour over all the
breasts, then cook for 1½ hours at 350 degrees.

The Secret? Wood & Sauce

Some of the finest smoked game I've tasted came from the
ovens of Grady Upshaw of Snug Harbor, Oklahoma. He and
his wife, Etta, own and operate Smokehouse Bar-B-Que No. 1
on Snug Harbor Road, 10 miles northeast of Wagoner,
Oklahoma, and Smokehouse No. 2 in Wagoner, which is
about 50 miles east of Tulsa.

Grady has huge smoking "pits" at both sites, preparing more
than 60,000 pounds of meat a year for his customers.

Grady's reputation as a smoke-cook has spread far and
wide, while he has smoked wild game, commercially, for a
large number of hunters.

He also makes the finest barbecue sauce (which he calls
Grady's Meat Sauce) that I've experienced. The recipe is

secret, but he sells the sauce commercially through his restaurants and to grocery outlets throughout the state, and by mail, UPS or Federal Express delivery anywhere in the nation.

He uses four ricks of wood per month at the two restaurants, cooking on huge metal racks inside concrete black and brick ovens.

"The secret to fixing fine ribs is the wood," Grady said. "I use six or seven sticks per day in each oven, two thirds hickory and one third sassafras."

I had never before heard of using sassafras as a cooking wood. Why would he use it?

"It's red inside, and it gives ribs and wild game meat a beautiful red color," he said, removing a mammoth tray of ribs hot and steaming from an oven.

He added that both hickory and sassafras are plentiful in his area, and he buys all his wood from local suppliers at about $50 a rick (4X8X2-feet, stacked).

"If you want really good food, every time, from any good smoker, use good wood, and have it going (burning) and the smoker filled with smoke before you put the meat in it," Grady said.

He added that it's a smart chef who adds a good barbecue sauce (or meat sauce) to the meat while it's smoking.

However, the sauce should not be placed on the meat until the last 20 minutes of cooking time, whether it's "wet" or "dry" smoking.

In service to hunters, Grady specializes in smoking venison, bear, elk, wild turkeys, rabbits and squirrels, geese and ducks.

"I even did a possum once," he said. "With a little sauce, it was fantastic."

If you'd like to visit with Grady about smoking, or his sauce, he can be reached at Smokehouse No. 1, Rt. 4, Box 175, Wagoner, OK 74467, (918) 462-7515 or Smokehouse No. 2, 621 West Cherokee, Wagoner, OK 74467, (918) 485-4140.

Wild Turkey Supreme

Serves: 10-15
Prep Time: 9 hours

1 12-16 lb. wild turkey
1 onion, peeled
4 sprigs parsley
4 strips bacon
2 carrots, peeled
1 separated head garlic, unpeeled

Preheat water smoker or start fire with full pan of charcoal. Pat turkey dry inside and out. Stuff cavity with onion, parsley and carrots. Sew and truss. Place bacon over turkey breast.

When fire is ready, add green or pre-soaked hickory chips or chunks. Put filled water pan in place and add garlic cloves to water.

Place turkey on food grid and keep temperature constant at about 200 to 225 degrees. Cook for 6½ to 8½ hours, depending on size of turkey. Bird is done when internal temperature reads 180 degrees.

VERSATILE FILM CANISTERS—REMEMBER ALL THOSE PLASTIC FILM CANISTERS YOU'VE BEEN SQUIRRELING AWAY, KNOWING THAT SOMEDAY THEY'D BE GOOD FOR SOMETHING? YOU WERE RIGHT. THE SMALL SIZE AND TIGHT SEAL OF 35MM FILM CANISTERS LET YOU TAKE ALONG THINGS YOU WOULDN'T DARE TOSS IN YOUR PACK. CLEAN 'EM AND FILL 'EM WITH BUTTER, PEANUT BUTTER OR CREAM CHEESE. USE THEM TO KEEP MATCHES DRY, AND SPICES FROM SPILLING.

Pecan-Stuffed Smoked Pheasant

Serves: 6
Prep Time: smoking time plus 2 hours

2 smoked pheasants
¼ cup butter
1⅓ cups dry bread crumbs
⅔ cup coarsely broken pecan meats
2 T. flour
¾ tsp. salt
¼ tsp. pepper
¼ cup butter
1½ cups hot water
⅓ cup sherry

Melt half the butter and pour over bread crumbs. Add pecan meats and toss lightly. Stuff mixture into pheasants and truss birds. Combine the flour, salt and pepper, and lightly sprinkle over pheasants. Melt the other butter in a heavy frying pan. Brown each pheasant on all sides and transfer to a roasting pan. Add hot water and sherry to the browned birds. Cover and bake at 350 degrees for 1 hour.

Baste with liquid every 15 minutes. Remove cover and continue baking for 20 minutes, or until the birds are crisp and brown. Remove birds to a platter and keep hot while you thicken drippings for gravy. Serves 6.

Luhr-Jensen & Sons

BUNS AND BREAD STICKS—TURN LEFTOVER HOT DOG BUNS INTO BREAD STICKS BY SPLITTING THE BUNS LENGTHWISE, THEN CUTTING EACH HALF INTO THREE STICKS. BUTTER LIBERALLY AND SPRINKLE WITH SHREDDED CHEESE. PLACE UNDER THE BROILER AND TOAST.

Duck A L'Orange

Serves: 3-4
Prep Time: 8 hours

4-5 lb. duck
1 cup orange juice
1 T. grated orange peel
1 cup Sauterne or other white wine
1 tsp. garlic, onion or celery salt
1 onion, quartered
1 apple, quartered
3 stalks celery, including leaves, sliced

Put duck in large, heavy duty plastic bag or deep bowl.
Combine orange juice and peel, wine and salt and pour over.
Close bag or cover bowl and refrigerate several hours or
overnight, turning duck occasionally. Lift from marinade. Put
onion, apple and celery in cavity; put on cooking grill. Pour
marinade into water pan. Smoke-cook about 6 to 8 hours or
until leg can be moved easily in joint. Use juices in water pan
for sauce. Try this marinade on goose, too. Charcoal models:
use full pan of briquettes, full water pan (including marinade).

Brinkman Corporation

Appetizer Ribs

Cut slabs of ribs crosswise into short (2- or 3-inch) lengths.
Marinate several hours or overnight in soy sauce, bottled
teriyaki sauce, bottled barbecue sauce or your very own sauce.
Arrange strips of ribs on cooking grill or in rib rack and
smoke-cook 2½ to 3½ hours or until meat begins to pull away
from bone. Remove from unit and cut between ribs with sharp
knife or kitchen shears before serving. Plan on ½ pound per
person as an appetizer.

Brinkmann Corporation

Sportsman's Sauce

Serves: varies
Prep Time: 30 minutes

1 16-oz. can tomato sauce
¼ cup Worcestershire sauce
juice from two limes
1 12-oz. bottle hot or regular catsup
2 tsp. Kitchen Bouquet sauce
1 T. prepared mustard
1 T. chili powder
1 onion, finely chopped
1 tsp. garlic powder
1 bottle beer
½ cup butter or margarine
Tabasco sauce to taste

Mix and simmer for 15 to 20 minutes.

Brinkmann Corporation

Venison Marsala

Serves: 12-15
Prep. Time: 10 hours

7-9 lb. venison roast
½-¾ lb. bacon
2-3 pinches rosemary leaves
2 beef bouillon cubes
1-1½ cups Marsala wine

Lay bacon strips over roast in crosshatch pattern. Be generous with bacon. Tie bacon onto roast with twine. Then use meat baster to force Marsala wine between bacon and roast. Again, be generous. Pour remaining wine over roast and into water pan.

Brinkmann Corporation

Roast Duck

Serves: 6-8
Prep Time: 6 hours

4 ducks
salt and pepper to taste
2 lg. onions, chopped
2 pared carrots, cut in half crosswise
2 stalks celery, chopped
2 apples, cored and chopped
¼ cup flour
2 (10½-oz. cans) consomme
½ cup dry sherry

Allow ducks to stand in salted water ½ hour. Remove from water and dry with a towel. Rub generously with salt and pepper. Stuff cavities with part of vegetables. Place ducks in a pan. Arrange remaining vegetables around ducks. Smoke for 1 hour. Dust ducks with flour. Add consomme, 1 soup can water and ½ cup dry sherry. Continue smoking for about 3½ hours or until done. Strain pan juice and add more sherry, if desired.

Brinkmann Corporation

POWDER POWER—IF YOUR BAKING POWDER HAS BEEN SITTING ON THE SHELF FOR SOME TIME, IT'S A GOOD IDEA TO CHECK ITS BAKING POWER BEFORE USING. PUT A SMALL AMOUNT IN A SAUCER AND ADD A LITTLE WATER. IT HAS LOST ITS LEAVENING POWER IF IT DOESN'T FIZZ.

Wild, Wild Game Jerky

Serves: varies
Prep Time: 24 hours

> **5 lbs. wild game meat**
> **¼ cup salt**
> **¼ cup sugar**
> **2 cups water**
> **1 cup cider**
> **1 cup soy sauce**
> **1 oz. bourbon or brandy**
> **½ tsp. onion powder**
> **½ tsp. garlic powder**
> **1 tsp. MSG**
> **1 tsp. grated fresh ginger**
> **1 tsp. grated orange peel**
> **6 white cloves**

Trim all fat from meat. Slice meat with the grain about ¼- to ½-inch thick. The meat slices nicely when semi-frozen. Mix the remaining ingredients together for marinade. Place meat in the cool marinade and leave overnight, or for no less than 8 hours.

Remove from marinade and allow to air dry without rinsing. Smoke for 12 to 16 hours, depending on how dry you like the jerky. Use 3 panfuls of Hickory or Cherry "Chips 'N Chunks" in the early stages of the drying cycle.

Luhr-Jensen & Sons

DELICIOUS DILL VEGETABLES—ADD RAW CUCUMBER AND CARROT STRIPS, STRING BEANS AND CAULIFLOWERS TO THE LIQUID LEFT IN A DILL PICKLE JAR. REFRIGERATE FOR SEVERAL DAYS TO MAKE DELICIOUS DILL-FLAVORED SNACKS.

Game Jerky

Serves: varies
Prep Time: 24 hours

> **5 lbs. wild game meat**
> **⅓ cup sugar**
> **¼ cup salt**
> **2 cups soy sauce**
> **1 cup water**
> **1 cup red wine**
> **½ tsp. onion powder**
> **½ tsp. pepper**
> **½ tsp. garlic powder**
> **½ tsp. Tabasco sauce**

Trim all fat from meat and follow same directions as "Wild, Wild Game Jerky" on previous page.

Luhr-Jensen & Sons

Easy Meat Jerky

Serves: varies
Prep Time: 25 hours

> **5 lbs. wild game meat**
> **½ cup non-iodized salt**
> **½ cup sugar**
> **1 qt. water**

Trim all fat from the meat. Slice meat *with* the grain as thin as possible. The meat slices nicely when semi-frozen. Place the meat in cool brine and refrigerate overnight.

After no less than 12 hours, take the meat from the brine, rinse lightly and allow to dry on paper towels for 1 hour.

Place meat strips on the smoker racks and dry for 12 hours, using 2 panfuls of Alder Chips 'n Chunks in the early stages of the drying cycle.

Luhr-Jensen & Sons

117

Smoked Duck A L'Orange (2 Ducks)

Serves: varies
Prep Time: smoking time plus 3 hours

2 ducks
flour
butter
1 cup white table wine
1 bay leaf
1 sm. onion
1 tsp. salt
1 sprig parsley
3 peppercorns
2 oranges

Cut the smoked birds in pieces and rub with flour. Cook in butter until lightly browned. Add wine, bay leaf, onion, salt, parsley and peppercorns. Cover and cook slowly until tender.

Remove duck to a warm platter. Strain sauce, adding the juice and the shredded zest (outer peel) of 2 oranges. Pour back on duck, heat and serve garnished with sliced peeled oranges.

Luhr-Jensen & Sons

CAREFULLY STORE DRIED HERBS—STORE DRIED HERBS IN COVERED GLASS JARS AWAY FROM HEAT AND STEAM. PURCHASE HERBS IN SMALL QUANTITIES AND USE WITHIN ONE YEAR.

Upland Bird

Hearty upland bird recipes for hungry NAHC members. Try "Creamed Dove Casserole" (page 120), "Grouse Supreme" (page 124) and "Smothered Quail" (page 134) for succulent meals.

Creamed Dove Casserole

Serves: 3-4
Prep Time: 1 hour

6-8 dove breasts
1 tsp. butter
1 10-oz. can cream of chicken soup
1 T. butter or margarine
salt and pepper to taste
¼ cup milk
¼ cup mushrooms, thinly sliced

Brush dove breasts with a small amount of butter and brown in casserole dish in hot oven. Cream together soup, butter, seasonings and milk. Pour over browned doves. Sprinkle with sliced mushrooms, cover and bake at 300 degrees for 45 minutes to 1 hour.

B. Lewandowski
Greenlane, Pennsylvania

HERBS & SPICES SHOULD BE ADDED LATER—IN FOODS THAT ARE LONG-COOKING, SUCH AS STEWS, ADD HERBS & SPICES DURING THE LAST HALF HOUR OF COOKING TIME SO THAT THE FLAVOR AND AROMA AREN'T LOST.

Dove Brandon

Serves: 2-3
Prep Time: 1 hour

4-6 dove breasts
    olive oil
¼ lb. butter
½ tsp. garlic powder
1½ tsp. parsley flakes
½ tsp. salt
½ tsp. pepper
½ tsp. nutmeg
½ tsp. celery salt
½ cup lemon or orange juice
1-3 dashes bitters
    cooking sherry (optional)
½ cup fresh mushrooms, sliced

Brown breasts in a small amount of olive oil. Drain. Melt butter and add seasonings and juice. Stir until thoroughly mixed. Add bitters and sherry to taste. Place breasts in a covered baking dish and pour butter mixture over them making sure that all meat is covered. Add mushroom slices. Bake at 325 degrees for approximately 45 minutes or until dove is tender. Be sure to keep the baking dish covered to prevent dove from drying out. Serve dove and sauce over egg noodles.

George Swartzfager
Brandon, Florida

MARINE BIRDS MAY TASTE FISHY—TO REMOVE THE FISHY TASTE OF MARINE BIRDS, SOAK THEM OVERNIGHT IN SALT OR VINEGAR WATER.

Dove-Kabobs

Serves: varies
Prep Time: 1½ hours

2-3 dove breasts per person
teriyaki sauce
3 med. onions
cherry tomatoes
mushrooms
1 lg. bell pepper

← *IF YOU LIKE 'EM HOT, ADD JALAPENO PEPPERS!*

Marinate breasts in teriyaki sauce for 1 hour. Save the sauce. Quarter onions. Cut bell pepper into 2-inch chunks. Skewer all ingredients on wooden skewers, alternating them. Barbecue until dove is tender, basting with sauce.

George Swartzfager
Brandon, Florida

Boogie Dove

← *GOOD WITH RED WINE OR COLD BEER!*

Serves: 4
Prep Time: overnight plus 2 hours

20 dove breasts
2 quarts water
8½ cups Worcestershire sauce
garlic spread
lemon pepper
bacon

Soak dove breasts in mixture of water and Worcestershire sauce for 4 hours or overnight. Place dove breasts on cookie sheet, cover with garlic spread and sprinkle each with dash of lemon pepper. Bake at 250 degrees for ½ hour. Place bacon strips on each breast and bake at 250 degrees for 1 hour. Serve on bed of wild rice. Garnish with parsley.

Ron Ladigo
Glendale, Arizona

Country Style Dove

Serves: 6
Prep Time: 1 hour

QUAIL ALSO TASTES GOOD THIS WAY!

20-30 dove breasts
1 lb. bacon
salt and pepper
1 med. onion, thinly sliced
3 egg yolks
2 cups half and half
1 tsp. sweet Hungarian paprika

In a large skillet, cook bacon until crisp. Drain on paper towels. Place sliced onion and doves in the skillet and brown in the bacon fat. Salt and pepper the birds. Remove birds and onions from skillet and place in a warm oven (about 150 to 200 degrees). Pour off all but 3 tablespoons of bacon fat. Mix the egg yolks and the half and half. Add mixture to the bacon fat in the skillet and cook over low heat just to thicken, stirring constantly. Do not boil. Stir in paprika and serve sauce with dove and fried potatoes.

William Ortez
Copperas Cove, Texas

CRUST THE WAY YOU LIKE IT—IF YOU WANT A SHINY, TENDER CRUST ON YOUR BREAD, RUB THE TOPS OF THE HOT LOAVES WITH UNSALTED SHORTENING. IF YOU WANT HARD, CHEWY CRUST, BRUSH THE WARM CRUST WITH WARM WATER.

Grouse Supreme

Serves: 6
Prep Time: 1½ hours

> **3 grouse**
> **½ cup flour**
> **2 T. parsley, dried**
> **2 T. ginger, ground**
> **2 T. paprika**
> **1 T. dry mustard**
> **½ tsp. course black pepper**
> **4 T. walnut oil**
> **4 T. margarine**
> **½ cup honey**
> **2 T. Worcestershire sauce**
> **¾ cups Madeira wine**

Split birds in half. Season flour with 1 tablespoon parsley, 1 tablespoon ginger, 1 tablespoon paprika, 1 tablespoon dry mustard and ½ teaspoon black pepper. Roll dry birds in seasoned flour, shaking off excess. Heat walnut oil and lightly brown each bird. Remove birds and set aside. Strain walnut oil remaining in first pan and pour into separate sauce pan. Add margarine. Melt over low heat. Add honey and dissolve. Stir in 1 tablespoon parsley, 1 tablespoon ginger and 1 tablespoon paprika. Add Worcestershire sauce. Stir for 2 minutes, add Madeira. Continue to stir until near boiling point. Add seasoned flour to thicken as you like it. Do *not* let sauce boil. Turn birds breast down in roasting pan. Pour sauce over and cook at 350 degrees for 20 minutes in oven. Reduce heat to 200 degrees for another 20 minutes. Remove, turn birds breast up. Place back in oven for another 10 minutes at 300 degrees or until brown.

H. F. Henriques
Orr, Minnesota

Breast Of Grouse

Serves: 3-4
Prep Time: 45 minutes

> 2 **breasts of grouse, halved**
> 4 **T. butter**
> ½ **jar tart jelly**
> 5 **oz. dry sherry**
>   **salt and pepper**
> 3-4 **T. heavy cream**
>   **paprika**

Saute breasts in butter until nearly tender. Add jelly and wine.
Salt and pepper to taste. Cook covered for 15 to 20 minutes.
Remove breasts to a platter. Add cream and a dash of paprika
to the gravy. Taste for seasoning and add more salt and
pepper if necessary. Pour gravy over meat.

John Lee
Osceola, Wisconsin

Broiled Woodcock

Serves: 4
Prep Time: 15 minutes

> 4 **woodcock**
>   **salt, pepper to taste**
> 4 **slices bacon**
> ¼ **cup butter, melted**
> 1 **T. parsley, chopped**
> 4 **slices buttered toast**

Sprinkle woodcock with salt and pepper. Wrap with bacon and
fasten with toothpicks. Place in broiler pan about 6 inches from
heat. Broil 8 to 10 minutes on each side or until tender, basting
frequently with butter. Sprinkle with parsley.

Robert Henderson
New Brunswick, Canada

Patti Farrell's Grouse With Pear Sauce

Serves: 2-3
Prep Time: 50 minutes

4 ruffed grouse breast halves, skin removed
¼ oz. dry white wine
1 16-oz. can pear halves in light syrup
½ cup whipping cream
2 T. flour
¾ cup reserved broth
¼ tsp. salt

Preheat oven to 325 degrees, line 9x9x2-inch baking pan with heavy duty foil, leaving ½-inch foil collar. Place grouse halves in pan. Pour wine and juice from pears over grouse; reserve pear halves. Place a sheet of foil over pan and fold edges together to form a tight seal. Bake 30 minutes or until meat tests done. Uncover. Remove ¾ cup of broth and set aside. Place pears around grouse in pan; bake 5 minutes longer or until fruit is heated. In saucepan, stir whipping cream into flour until thickened. Add reserved broth and salt and heat thoroughly. Remove grouse and pears to platter. To serve, spoon sauce over grouse.

James Farrell, Sr.
Portland, New York

STUFFING AND LEFTOVERS—COOL DRESSING BEFORE STUFFING YOUR BIRD. REMOVE DRESSING BEFORE REFRIGERATING LEFTOVERS.

Quick-N-Easy Partridge

Serves: 6
Prep Time: 1 hour

> **3 partridge breasts**
> **2 eggs**
> **2 T. milk**
> **2-3 cups seasoned croutons**
> **flour**
> **margarine or shortening**

Fillet the partridge breasts. Slice each half into 2 pieces. Beat eggs and milk together. Crush croutons. Dry the breast pieces. Roll each piece in flour, then dip into the egg mixture and roll in croutons. Fry in margarine or butter flavor shortening. Fry at 350 degrees until browned and done.

Gary Nelson
Rib Lake, Wisconsin

Sauteed Partridge Slices

Serves: 1-2
Prep Time: 30 minutes

> **1 partridge breast**
> **1 cup flour**
> **½ tsp. paprika**
> **salt**
> **pepper**
> **2 T. butter**

Thoroughly clean partridge breast and remove skin. Cut into thin slices. Dip each slice of meat in mixture of flour, paprika, salt and pepper. Preheat a heavy skillet, preferably cast iron. Slowly saute breast slices in butter over low heat until crisp and golden brown, about 14 to 16 minutes on each side. Serve with your favorite salad, vegetables and potato.

Robert Henderson
New Brunswick, Canada

Phineas' Partridge Pie

Serves: 3-4
Prep Time: 2-3 hours

> **3 partridge**
> **½ lb. veal, cut ½-inch thick**
> **1¼ tsp. salt**
> **⅛ tsp. pepper**
> **6 bacon slices**
> **¼ cup bacon fat**
> **1 T. salad oil**
> **3 T. flour**
> **2 cups bouillon**
> **2 whole cloves**
> **1 cup mushrooms, sliced**
> **2 T. butter or margarine**
> **1 T. parsley, chopped**
> **sherry**
> **flaky pastry**

Cut partridge in half lengthwise. Slice veal into six strips. Sprinkle partridge and veal with 1 teaspoon salt and ⅛ teaspoon of pepper. Cut bacon slices in half and saute until golden brown. Put partridge in bottom of 2-quart casserole and cover with veal and bacon. Add 1 tablespoon salad oil to bacon fat in skillet and gradually add 3 tablespoons flour. Stir in 2 cups bouillon and cook until thick. Add cloves and remaining ¼ teaspoon salt and pour over meat. Cover and bake at 350 degrees for 1 hour. Meanwhile, saute mushrooms in butter until tender. Place mushrooms and parsley over ingredients in casserole. Pour sherry over all and top with your favorite flaky pastry dough rolled to ⅛-inch thickness. Bake uncovered at 450 degrees until pastry is light brown.

Phineas Lea
Auburn, Georgia

Pheasant In Spiced Sour Cream

Serves: 4
Prep Time: 2 hours

   1 **pheasant, cut up**
     flour
     butter
   1 **8-oz. carton sour cream**
  16 **oz. water**
     Worcestershire sauce to taste
     few drops Tabasco sauce
 1-2 **bay leaves**
     dash sweet basil
     dash rosemary
     salt and pepper

Dust pieces of pheasant with flour and brown in butter. Mix
sour cream and water. Add remaining ingredients to sour
cream mixture. Pour sour cream mixture in a covered roaster
and add pheasant. Steam for several hours at 325 degrees until
tender.

Bob Kolde
St. Marys, Kansas

NOT TOO MUCH—WHEN ADDING HERBS IT IS BETTER TO USE TOO
LITTLE THAN TOO MUCH.

Mexican Pheasant

Serves: 6-8
Prep Time: 1 hour

2 cups cooked pheasant, cut in 1-inch bites
1 can cream of mushroom soup
1 can cream of chicken soup
1 onion, chopped
½ jar medium salsa
1 cup sour cream
1 cup cheddar cheese, grated
1 cup Monterey Jack cheese, grated
1 pkg. corn tortillas, cut in strips

Combine pheasant, soups, onion, salsa, sour cream and ¾ cheese. Layer mixture with tortilla strips. Top with remaining cheese. Bake 30 minutes at 350 degrees.

Peter Carlson
Kensington, California

Mandarin Pheasant

Serves: 6
Prep Time: 2 hours

2 pheasants, halved
1 11-oz. can mandarin oranges
1 T. cornstarch
2 tsp. grated lemon peel
1 T. lemon juice

Drain oranges, draining syrup into pan. Stir in cornstarch, lemon peel and juice. Cook until thickened, stirring constantly. Remove from heat; add oranges. Place pheasant breast-side up in baking pan. Spoon sauce over birds and cover. Bake 15 minutes at 425 degrees. Bake 1 hour 325 degrees, baste often. Remove cover. Bake 30 minutes.

Stephen Kaminski
Derry, New Hampshire

Pheasant Paprika

Serves: 4-6
Prep Time: 1 hour

1 **3-lb. pheasant**
1 **onion, chopped**
4 **T. shortening**
1 **T. paprika**
¾ **tsp. black pepper**
1 **T. salt**
1½ **cups water**
½ **cup stewed tomatoes**
½ **pint sour cream**
2 **cups flour**
2 **eggs**
½ **tsp. salt**
½ **cup water**

FOR MORE GRAVY, ADD ½ PINT SWEET CREAM TO SOUR CREAM!

Brown onion in shortening, add pheasant and seasonings; brown 10 minutes. Add water and tomatoes, cover and let simmer slowly until tender. Remove pheasant; add sour cream to the drippings in pan and mix well. For dumplings, combine flour, eggs and salt. Add water. Beat well until the dough is gummy. Drop by teaspoon into boiling water. Boil 2 minutes. Drain. Rinse with hot water. Add dumplings to gravy and arrange pheasant on top. Heat through and serve.

Mrs. Pamela Nagy
Milford, Michigan

SEPARATE BACON SLICES EASILY—TO SEPARATE FROZEN BACON SLICES QUICKLY WITHOUT BREAKING THEM, ROLL UP THE ENTIRE PACKAGE DIAGONALLY BEFORE YOU OPEN IT.

Patti Farrell's Pheasants Jubilee

Serves: 4-6
Prep Time: 2 hours

> 2 **3-lb. pheasants**
> **salt**
> 2 **apples, quartered**
> 1 **lg. onion, sliced**
> **celery leaves**
> 6 **slices bacon**
> 1 **T. cornstarch**
> 1 **16-oz. can pitted sweet cherries**
> ¼ **cup dry white wine**
> ¼ **tsp. salt**
> 1 **T. margarine**

Wash birds, pat dry. Lightly salt cavities and stuff each with quartered apples, onions and celery leaves. Cover each bird with slices of bacon. Wrap in foil and roast in shallow pan at 375 degrees for 1½ hours. Last ½ hour, remove foil to allow birds to brown. Remove from oven and set aside 1 tablespoon drippings. Discard stuffing. To make Jubilee sauce, combine reserved drippings and cornstarch in a small saucepan. Drain cherries, reserving syrup. Combine reserved syrup, wine and ¼ teaspoon salt; stir into cornstarch mixture. Cook and stir until sauce thickens and bubbles. Stir in cherries and margarine; heat through. Makes 2½ cups of sauce. Carve pheasants and serve with Jubilee sauce.

James Farrell, Sr.
Portland, New York

A TASTIER BAKED POTATO—MAKE SMALL HOLES IN BAKED POTATO WITH A FORK WHEN IT'S HALF-COOKED TO ALLOW THE STEAM TO ESCAPE. POTATO WILL TASTE MUCH BETTER.

Joe Mahma Quail

Serves: 4
Prep Time: 1 hour

GREAT WITH
BEANS AND FOOTBALL!

> **20 quail breasts**
> **Italian dressing**
> **Shake'n Bake for chicken**
> **lemon pepper**

Soak quail in Italian dressing for 20 minutes. Coat each with Shake'n Bake and place on cookie sheet. Sprinkle with lemon pepper. Bake at 350 degrees for 40 minutes.

Ron Ladigo
Glendale, Arizona

Beth's Baked Quail

Serves: 6
Prep Time: overnight plus 1 hour

> **12 quail breasts**
> **1 can evaporated milk**
> **2 eggs**
> **2 cups corn flakes**
> **1 baking bag**

Pour 1 can of evaporated milk over quail and refrigerate overnight. Beat 2 eggs in bowl and crush corn flakes in another bowl. Dip quail pieces in egg and then corn flakes. Place in baking bag in shallow pan and bake until brown about 45 minutes at 350 degrees.

Jay Conner
Topeka, Kansas

Sauteed Quail

Serves: varies
Prep Time: ½ hour

4 quail, halved
½ cup butter
½ cup dry white wine
¼ tsp. paprika
¼ cup chopped parsley
salt and pepper to taste

Melt butter in a Dutch oven. Add quail, browning on all sides.
Add wine and seasonings. Reduce heat and cover. Gently cook
for 8 to 12 minutes until tender.

Tom Squier
Aberdeen, North Carolina

Smothered Quail

Serves: varies
Prep Time: 1½ hours

6 whole quail
1 stick butter
4 T. flour
2 cups chicken stock
½ cup dry sherry
¾ tsp. chopped parsley
½ tsp. chervil (optional)
salt and pepper to taste

GRAVY IS EXCELLENT OVER RICE!

Brown quail in melted butter. Remove to a casserole. Slowly
stir flour into butter in skillet. Combine chicken stock, sherry
and herbs and add to flour mixture. Pour over quail. Salt and
pepper to taste. Cover casserole and bake at 350 degrees for
an hour.

Tom Squier
Aberdeen, North Carolina

Waterfowl

Favorite duck and goose recipes. Serve up satisfying meals with these recipes from your fellow NAHC members.

Marinated Duck

Serves: 4
Prep Time: overnight plus 2 hours

2 ducks
½ cup soy sauce
2 T. sugar
½ cup dry red wine
1 sm. onion, chopped
1 tsp. ground ginger
2 garlic cloves, minced
2 bay leaves, crumbled

Cut ducks in half lengthwise. Place in plastic bag in shallow
pan. Combine remaining ingredients and pour over duck.
Cover and marinate overnight in refrigerator, turning
occasionally. Preheat oven to 425 degrees. Remove ducks from
marinade and place skin side up in 13x19-inch pan. Bake
uncovered, 15 minutes. Reduce temperature to 325 degrees.
Pour marinade over ducks and cover lightly. Bake 1 to 1½
hours or until tender. Occasionally baste with marinade.

Stephen Kaminski
Derry, New Hampshire

STORING YEAST DOUGH—ANY YEAST DOUGH CONTAINING AT
LEAST 1 TABLESPOON OF SUGAR PER CUP OF FLOUR CAN BE
REFRIGERATED UP TO 3 DAYS. IMMEDIATELY AFTER KNEADING, GREASE
TOP OF DOUGH AND COVER WITH WAXED PAPER OR PLASTIC WRAP, THEN
A DAMP CLOTH. REFRIGERATE UNTIL READY TO USE. REMOVE TWO HOURS
BEFORE BAKING.

Wild Roast Duck

Serves: 4
Prep Time: 1 hour

- **2 mallard ducks**
- **1 cup celery chunks**
- **1 cup carrot chunks**
- **1 cup onion chunks**
- **½ cup melted butter** ← *REAL BUTTER IS BEST!*
- **½ cup Worcestershire sauce**
- **¼ cup cooking oil**
- **1 T. salt**

Place your black cast iron pot in the oven with the lid on. Set oven to highest temperature and heat pot thoroughly. Clean ducks and salt well inside and out. Stuff with large chunks of celery, carrot and onion. Remove heated pot from the oven ad rub inside with oil. Place ducks in pot. Replace lid and return to oven. Oven should still be set to highest temperature. Do not peek, baste or even open the oven door for 1 hour. When the hour is up remove ducks from the oven and make a slit in each side of the breasts and pour on melted butter and Worcestershire. I guarantee if you follow these directions exactly you will have the brownest, juiciest, most tender duck you've ever eaten.

Joanne Franklin
Rocklin, California

COOK DUCKS RARE—THE FLAVOR IS BEST WHEN DUCKS ARE COOKED RARE.

Roasted Goose

Serves: 4
Prep Time: 3-4 hours

> 1 **goose, cleaned**
> 1 **lg. oven roaster bag**
> ¼ **cup celery, diced**
> ¼ **cup fresh onions, sliced**
> 1 **package dry chicken broth (boullion)**
> ¾ **cup hot water**
> **salt, pepper and parsley to taste**
> 4-5 **slices smoked dried beef**

Place goose in roaster bag. Combine celery, onions, chicken broth and water. Pour mixture over goose and inside cavity. Lay slices of dried beef over top of goose. Seal bag. Bake at 250 degrees for 3 to 4 hours. Remove from roaster bag and gently peel outer darkened skin. Meat will be tender and will pull away from bone if fully cooked.

B. Lewandowski
Greenlane, Pennsylvania

FRESHER SPICES—REFRIGERATE CHILI POWDER, PAPRIKA AND CAYENNE PEPPER TO KEEP THEM FRESH LONGER.

Barbecued Duck

Serves: 3-4
Prep Time: 1 hour

> 2 **mallards** ←
> ½ **lb. butter**
> ½ **cup catsup**
> 1 **T. sugar**
> 1½ **T. lemon juice**
> 1 **T. Worcestershire sauce**
>   **ground pepper**
> 1 **tsp. salt**
> 1 **garlic clove, pressed**
> 1 **sm. onion, chopped**
> ½ **tsp. Tabasco sauce**

OR USE 4 WOOD DUCKS!

Mix ingredients for sauce. Cover and simmer 5 to 10 minutes. Apply liberally over ducks and grill until done to your liking.

Randy Hilliard
Warren, Ohio

BARBECUE FOR BETTER FLAVOR—OUTDOOR BARBECUE GRILLING COMPLEMENTS THE FLAVOR OF GAME.

Cleo's Roast Goose With Apple Stuffing

Serves: 6
Prep Time: 4-5 hours

   1 **goose**
   1 **tsp. salt**
   1 **tsp. pepper**
   3 **cups apples, diced**
 ½ **cup water**
1½ **cups onions, chopped**
   1 **tsp. celery seed**
 ¾ **cup butter, melted**
 ¾ **cup apple cider**
   6 **cups toasted bread crumbs**
   4 **slices bacon**

BE SURE TO REMOVE ALL FAT FROM GOOSE!

Soak goose in salt water ½ hour. Drain and wipe dry. Rub inside and outside with salt and pepper. Prick breast, legs and wings with a fork. Cook apples in ½ cup water. Cook onions and celery seed in butter for 3 minutes. Mix apples, onions, apple cider, celery seed, salt and pepper with bread crumbs and stuff body and neck cavity. Place breast side up in shallow roasting pan. Lay 4 slices of bacon on top of goose. Roast uncovered at 325 degrees for 4 to 5 hours.

Kenneth Crummett
Sugar Grove, West Virginia

RAW POTATOES REMOVE WILD TASTE—TO TAKE THE GAMEY TASTE OUT OF GOOSE, STUFF THE CAVITY WITH QUARTERED RAW POTATOES. DISCARD THE POTATOES BEFORE SERVING.

Freeze It Right

Tips, techniques and recipes for freezing wild game. Freezing is perhaps the easiest way to preserve wild game at home. Well-known food specialists Annette and Louis Bignami show you how to be sure your food comes out of the freezer in the same good shape that it went into the freezer. Plus, you'll find recipes for meals that are easy to fix and freeze.

Freeze It Right!

by Annette & Louis Bignami

Freezing food has to be the safest and easiest way to preserve game at home. Since we eat game and game birds in place of domestic meats we take special care to ensure that the food we eat comes out of the freezer in the same good shape that it went in.

The mechanics of freezing are simple. What's most important is a careful consideration of portion size and future recipes so you don't face a whole frozen turkey when you just want breast meat to smoke. We also use the freezer to store extra servings of our favorite game and gamebird entrees (recipes to follow). This lets the cook spend more time hunting!

Freezing game starts with field care. Quick evisceration is a must. We pluck some birds and skin others. Since we freeze all birds except turkeys in water, we don't feel skin is necessary to retain moisture in frozen birds or in cooked dishes, except where birds are dry roasted or broiled. Birds cooked in a sauce don't dry out!

Arguments rage about how long you should hang game and game birds to tenderize them. We age birds in their feathers in the refrigerator for one to three days. We hang deer for a night or two; then bone. Since we live in California it's not possible to hang game and birds outdoors for longer periods. The weather is much too hot. At 40 to 50 degrees, hang it for a longer period.

We freeze small birds like quail four at a time in quart plastic milk containers. Some pheasants freeze whole in half-gallon containers. However, we portion most of our pheasants, sage grouse and turkeys. Breasts are individually wrapped and used for supremes. Legs and thighs go six or eight at a time, with shot up bird parts, into plastic milk cartons for later use in enchiladas, pasties and other dishes. We save backs and necks for stock. This is more flexible than freezing birds whole. Note: if you butcher-wrap birds, tuck the legs inside the body cavity for a compact package less likely to freezer-burn.

We bone big game. This eliminates bone chips and ensures compact packages that wrap and freeze in minimum space. Cutting game along muscle groups also makes the final result more uniform than is the case with steaks that might have tender and tough sections.

We don't waste bones. We roast them in a 400-degree oven, then boil them for stock that is reduced by 75 percent and frozen in ice cube trays. We save "good" trimmings for sausage or ground meat. "Bad" trimmings freeze for dog food.

Do freeze foods fast. Home freezers should operate below minus 12 degrees Fahrenheit. If food is frozen above minus 5 degrees, its food value, color and flavor are effected. Commercial freezers operate around minus 20 degrees; these are recommended if you freeze wild pigs.

However, you will not be able to keep freezer temperatures down to these levels if you add an entire deer or elk to the freezer all at once. The solution is to bone out the forequarters one day; then bone the hindquarters the next. Each day wrap meal-size portions—one- or two-pound packages—in pliofilm (clear plastic freezer wrap), then in double wrapped freezer paper and tape them tightly shut with freezer tape. Take care to remove as much air as possible when wrapping. Another good method puts game or game birds in plastic bags filled with water. Note: Try to wrap *all* packages as rectangular as possible so they fill the freezer with no wasted space.

Other packages work, too. Pliofilm, laminated polyethylene freezer paper, double zip-lock bags—which are wonderful for cooked dishes like stews—do the job. Plastic containers with snap-on lids work too. The key is to have an air-tight double wrap of moisture-proof paper that eliminates the oxidation and evaporation that causes "freezer burn." Just avoid regular wax paper or plastic wraps.

We add just *two pounds* of meat per cubic foot of freezer space per day until everything is frozen. This speeds up the freezing process so large ice crystals that damage meat cells do not form. Holding meat in the refrigerator substitutes for al fresco hanging, too.

Labels used to be a problem. Now we use a waterproof pen to mark the date, species, cut, weight and other information on the package's tape. For example, birds are marked "skin on" or "skin off" and "prime" or "shot up." We have a list of game posted to the freezer and try to check off packages as they are used. If you separate birds or game, put the newest packages in the back or bottom so nothing is kept too long.

Do thaw frozen foods slowly if possible. Overnight thawing in the refrigerator is the best bet. Small packages will thaw overnight; roasts might take 24 hours. Remember that partly thawed meats are easier to slice into thin cuts.

Storage life of frozen food varies. Experts claim you can keep roasts for a year, but you should use steaks in six months and variety or ground meat within two months. White flesh birds supposedly keep a year; game birds six months and giblets three months. We keep everything up to a year.

We find that freezer wrapped ducks lose a bit of taste and texture after six months. Those ducks that are frozen in water, meanwhile, seem to maintain their taste and texture longer. Ground meats were a problem. Now we freeze meat scraps in pound packages; then grind them just before we eat them. The only meats we freeze ground are cased sausages—casings cut down on evaporation and oxidation. Note, that fats pick up bad tastes and odors, so remove as much fat as you can.

It is possible to "refreeze" game and game birds. We often thaw, cook extra portions and refreeze the cooked leftovers. The recipes that follow are especially suited to this.

Don't fear substitutions either. If you don't have enough pheasant, toss in some quail or, if you like dark meat, use ducks. Deer, antelope, elk and caribou are reasonably interchangeable if you adjust your cooking times.

Pheasant Enchiladas

Serves: 6
Prep Time: 4 hours

   1 **pheasant, cut into pieces or 8 legs and thighs**
   2 **10-oz. cans enchilada sauce**
   2 **10-oz. cans red chili sauce**
   2 **med. onions, chopped**
   3 **hard-cooked eggs**
   2 **cups cheddar cheese, grated**
   2 **cups Monterey Jack cheese, grated**
   6 **oz. can of pitted black olives**
   4 **oz. can of diced green chiles**
   1 **dozen flour tortillas**

In a large saucepan, add pheasant pieces and one can of enchilada and chili sauce. Bring to a boil over medium heat, cover and simmer over low heat 2 to 3 hours or until pheasant is tender. Drain the pheasant and cool. Reserve the remaining sauce. Discard the skin and shred meat. In a small saucepan, cover the chopped onions with water, boil three minutes and drain. Chop hard-cooked eggs, mix grated cheeses, drain olives and place each in a separate dish. Reserve ½ cup cheese and a few olives for topping.

Heat oven to 350 degrees. Butter a 13X9-inch baking dish. Dip a tortilla into warm sauce to soften. Spoon 1/12 of the shredded meat and the fillings into each tortilla and tuck its edges under in a smooth roll. Repeat until side-by-side rolled tortillas fill the pan. Pour the remaining cans of enchilada and chili sauce over the top and sprinkle with the cheese and olives. Bake 40 minutes. Optional: Just before serving top with a spoonful of sour cream and/or guacamole.

This is an exellent way to stretch pheasant or to use older, tougher pieces. The recipe freezes and reheats well.

Gamebird Pasties

Serves: 12
Prep Time: 1½ hours

   4½ cups flour, sifted
    1 tsp. salt
    1 tsp. curry powder
   ½ tsp paprika
  24 T. vegetable shortening
  13 T. ice water
    2 cups cooked shredded duck and/or goose meat
    2 cups cooked shredded pheasant, grouse or quail meat
    3 cups potatoes in ½-inch cubes
    1 cup carrots, sliced
    1 onion, chopped
    1 tsp. thyme
    1 tsp. sage
   ½ tsp. salt
   ¼ tsp. pepper
   ⅓ cup dry white wine
    1 tsp. sugar
    2 T. flour
    2 med. tart apples, peeled and sliced
    1 egg white
    1 T. water

Crust. In a bowl, combine flour with salt, curry powder and paprika. Cut in shortening with a pastry blender or fork until well mixed and pea-sized. Add ice water one tablespoon at a time until well mixed; or use a food processor. Form into two balls, wrap in waxed paper and refrigerate 30 minutes.

Filling. In a large bowl, combine the duck, pheasant, potatoes, carrots, onions, thyme, sage, salt and pepper. On waxed paper mix the sugar with the flour. Dust the apple slices with the flour mixture. In a small bowl, beat egg white and water with a fork.

Heat oven to 375 degrees and lightly grease two cookie sheets. Divide the chilled dough ball rolls into 24 parts. On a lightly floured board, roll 12 parts into 6-inch circles. Place ¾ of the filling in the centers of these rounds, leaving a ½-inch wide edge. Top with the floured apple slices. Roll the other 12 dough balls into 7-inch circles to cover the filling. Pinch and flute edges. Brush crust with egg wash and bake about one hour or until golden brown.

This recipe makes 12 pasties you can freeze on cookie sheets, then wrap in freezer wrap or aluminum foil and freeze until needed. Leftover browned pasties reheat in the microwave or oven. We follow Cornish tradition and splash malt vinegar on newly opened piping-hot pasties.

Instant Game Teriyaki

Serves: 6
Prep Time: 15 minutes

> **2 lbs. boneless, tenderloin or other tender cut**
> **1¾ cups soy sauce**
> **1 tsp. garlic powder**
> **½ cup sugar**
> **1 T. grated fresh ginger root, optional**
> **1 T. oil**

Cut meat into ¼-inch thick slices. In a bowl, combine the soy sauce, garlic powder, sugar and ginger root. Heat a skillet over medium-high heat, add the oil and brown the meat, about 30 seconds on both sides. Stir in the soy sauce mixture and heat 30 seconds. Remove and serve on warm toasted rolls. Enjoy!

This dish will cook while rolls toast if you partly thaw meat in the microwave, slice it and thaw a minute more. It's a wonderful dish for shore or hunting camp lunches, too.

Game Chili Beans

Serves: varies
Prep Time: overnight plus 3 hours

 1 lb. red kidney beans
 3 strips thick bacon
 **2 lbs. game meat, venison, elk or antelope,
  diced or coarsely ground**
 2 16-oz. cans of stewed tomatoes, chopped
 1 12-oz. can of beer
 3 T. chili powder
 1 T. ground cumin
 1 T. dried oregano
 1 T. cocoa
 1 4-oz. can diced green chiles
 1 tsp. salt
 ½ tsp. pepper

In a large bowl, soak the beans overnight in enough water to cover. Cook the beans in a large saucepan over medium heat; add more water if needed. Cook about 1½ hours or until just tender. Rinse the beans with cold water and drain.

In a Dutch oven, cook the bacon until crisp, then remove bacon from pan; brown the meat in the bacon drippings. Add the tomatoes, beer, beans, chili powder, cumin, oregano, cocoa, green chiles, salt and pepper. Bring to a boil, lower the heat and cook 1½ hours. Add chili powder or salt and pepper to taste.

This dish warms winter hunters, adds a special touch to chili dogs, omelettes, tacos and goes very nicely with Mexican and Southwest dishes. You can portion and freeze it into one-cup servings. It reheats well. It's a great use for freezer-burned meat. You can also make it when you have "odds and ends" left in the freezer that you want to clear out before hunting season.

Venison Carbonade

Serves: 10
Prep Time: 3 hours

¼ **lb. salt pork, diced into ¼-inch pieces**
4 **med. yellow onions, thinly sliced**
1 **T. sugar**
1 **cup flour**
1 **T. thyme**
½ **tsp. salt**
½ **tsp. pepper**
3 **lbs. venison or other game, cut into ½-inch**
  pieces
1 **T. olive oil**
1 **T. butter**
1½ **T. brown sugar**
2 **cups dark beer**
1 **T. brown sugar**

In a Dutch oven, saute salt pork until brown and crisp, remove and set aside. Add the onions, cover and cook 20 minutes until tender over low heat. Uncover, add sugar, raise the heat, stir and cook until brown. Remove the onions and drain in a strainer.

In a plastic bag, combine the flour, thyme, salt and pepper. Add the venison pieces a few at a time, shake to coat.

To the Dutch oven, add the oil and butter, heat until hot. Add a few pieces of meat and brown on all sides. Do not overcrowd the meat when browning. Remove the meat as browned and continue until all the meat is browned, add more butter and oil if necessary. Return the meat and onions to the pan. Add the beer and brown sugar, cook over low heat about 2 hours or in a 325-degree oven. Taste and correct seasoning.

This makes a great winter meal! The combination of dark beer and onions with the crunch of salt pork complements the taste and texture of egg noodles. It freezes well and improves on reheating.

Pheasant Sausage

Serves: 10
Prep Time: 1 hour

   2 cups onions, diced
   ¾ cup milk
   ½ cup bread crumbs
   1 lb. fresh boned pheasant
   3 lbs. boneless pork butt
   2 tsp. salt
   2 tsp. white pepper
1½ tsp. allspice
   ½ tsp. nutmeg
   5 eggs
   4 oz. of sausage casings

In a saucepan, cover the onions with water and boil 5 minutes; then drain. Scald the milk with the bread crumbs; then cool.

Chop the pheasant and pork in a food processor using the steel blade. In a bowl, mix the pheasant, pork, onions, salt, pepper, allspice, nutmeg and the milk-soaked bread crumbs. Add the eggs one at a time and continue to mix well after each egg. Fill the sausage casings and twist into 6-inch links. Optional: Use a fine blade of a meat grinder to grind the pheasant and pork. The sausage filling can also be made into patties without using the sausage casings.

To cook, bring 1 quart of water and 2 cups of milk to a boil. Add about 12 links of sausage and simmer gently for 20 minutes. Serve plain or brush with melted butter and broil for 2 minutes until brown.

If you get late season preserve pheasants that are a bit soft, or simply have so many game birds you know you won't eat them during the year, try these wonderful sausages. We make batches with legs and backs, too. We freeze and enjoy this subtle sausage all year in sandwiches, omelettes and other dishes.

Small Game

Nineteen simple yet satisfying recipes for small game. Try "Down On Your Luck Hare" (page 154) or "Squirrel Gumbo" (page 166). Or add a new twist to an old dish with "Kentucky Fried Rabbit" (page 160) or "Barbecued Squirrel" (page 165).

Sweet And Sour Rabbit

Serves: 6
Prep Time: 30 minutes

> 3 cups cooked rabbit, diced
> ¼ cup brown sugar
> 2 T. corn starch
> ½ tsp. salt
> ¾ cup pineapple juice
> ¼ cup vinegar
> 1 T. soy sauce
> ¼ cup onion, sliced
> 1 cup drained pineapple
> ½ cup celery, chopped
> ½ cup green pepper, chopped
> 2 T. pimento, diced

Combine brown sugar, corn starch and salt. Stir in pineapple juice. Add vinegar and soy sauce. Boil, then reduce heat and cook until thick, stirring constantly. Remove from heat. Add rabbit, onion, pineapple, celery and green pepper. Cook 5 minutes. Add pimento and cook 1 minute more.

Alan Whitney
New Haven, Vermont

YOUNG RABBITS GOOD SUBSTITUTE—YOUNG RABBITS CAN BE PREPARED MUCH LIKE CHICKEN AND SUBSTITUTED IN MOST RECIPES THAT CALL FOR CHICKEN.

Rabbit With Grapefruit Juice

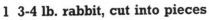

BEST SERVED WITH RICE OR POTATOES!

Serves: 4
Prep Time: 1-1½ hours

- **1 3-4 lb. rabbit, cut into pieces**
- **1 cup all purpose flour**
- **1 tsp. Season-All**
- **1 tsp. garlic powder**
- **¼ tsp. pepper**
- **¼ tsp. thyme**
- **½ tsp. salt**
  grapefruit juice
- **½ cup cooking oil**
- **1 med. onion, chopped**

Combine flour with seasonings. Dip each piece of rabbit in grapefruit juice, then roll it in flour mixture until meat is thoroughly coated. Save remaining grapefruit juice and seasoned flour. Pour the oil and chopped onion into a deep, heavy pot and heat over high flame. Place the floured rabbit in the pot and brown each piece on both sides. Lower the flame. Stir together the remaining grapefruit juice and flour mixture and add them to the pot. Cover and let simmer until meat is tender, turning rabbit pieces from time to time to keep from sticking.

Stephen Kaminski
Derry, New Hampshire

ADD COLOR TO YOUR DISH—THE MOST COLORFUL GARNISH YOU'LL FIND FOR A CASSEROLE MAY BE AN INGREDIENT IN THE DISH ITSELF. SAVE A FEW COOKED CARROT OR OLIVE SLICES, MUSHROOMS, OR SNIPPED PARSLEY TO SPRINKLE OVER THE CASSEROLE JUST BEFORE SERVING. OR, SLICE AN EXTRA TOMATO OR GREEN PEPPER TO ARRANGE ATOP THE DISH DURING THE LAST FEW MINUTES OF BAKING.

Down On Your Luck Hare

Serves: 4-6
Prep Time: 1½ hours

  2 rabbits, cut up
  2 cups hot water
  5 T. bacon fat
  5 chicken bouillon cubes
  1 can mushrooms
  1 tsp. parsley
  1 green pepper, sliced
  1 can green peas, drained
  1 sm. onion, chopped

Brown rabbit with the bacon fat. Dissolve bouillon cubes in hot water and add all the ingredients. Simmer for 45 minutes.

Rick Sinchak
Warren, Ohio

Barbecued Rabbit

Serves: 4-6
Prep Time: 1½ hours

  2-3 rabbits, cut up
    flour
    oil
    1 17-oz. can tomato sauce
  ⅔ cup brown sugar
  1½ T. liquid smoke
    1 tsp. hot chili powder

Roll rabbit in flour. Brown in a heavy skillet. Mix other ingredients, pour over rabbit. Simmer, tightly covered, for 45 minutes or until tender. Uncover skillet last 15 minutes.

Garth Carter
Cedar City, Utah

Rabbit And Dumplings

Serves: 4-6
Prep Time: 1½ hours

 2 **rabbits, cut up**
  flour
 6 **T. butter**
2½ **quarts water**
 1 **can tomatoes**
 1 **lg. onion, diced**
1½ **tsp. salt**
 ¼ **tsp. pepper**
 3 **cups flour**
 ¾ **tsp. salt**
 6 **tsp. baking powder**
1½ **cups milk**

Dredge rabbit in flour and brown in butter. Add rabbit and butter to large pot with water, tomatoes, onion, salt and pepper. Simmer until tender. For dumplings, sift together: 3 cups flour, ¾ teaspoon salt and 6 teaspoons baking powder. Add milk, blending until well moistened. Drop by spoonfuls into simmering rabbit stew. Cover and simmer gently 15 minutes with lid on.

Tom Squier
Aberdeen, North Carolina

STORING CASSEROLES—FREEZE CASSEROLE TOPPINGS SEPARATELY TO KEEP THEM FROM BECOMING SOGGY. KEEP A SUPPLY OF PLAIN OR BUTTERED CRUMBS IN THE FREEZER TO USE ON FROZEN CASSEROLES.

Hasenpfeffer

Serves: 4-6
Prep Time: 2½ hours

> **2 rabbits, cut up**
>   **flour**
> **½ cup olive oil**
> **1 lg. onion, chopped**
> **1½ cups tomato juice**
> **¾ cup wine vinegar or dry wine**
> **2 T. sugar**
> **2 T. pickling spices, tied in cheesecloth**

Roll rabbit pieces in flour and brown in olive oil. Remove rabbit from frying pan and place in large pot. In the frying pan braise chopped onion. Add tomato juice, wine and sugar. Simmer 2 minutes and pour over meat. Drop in bag of spices and cook 1 hour. Remove spices and simmer 1 more hour. Serve over noodles.

Tom Squier
Aberdeen, North Carolina

IF TOO THIN, THICKEN BY ADDING FLOUR!

AVOID THAT GREASY TASTE—ADD A TEASPOON OF VINEGAR TO THE FAT IN WHICH YOU ARE GOING TO DEEP FRY. IT WILL KEEP THE FOOD FROM ABSORBING TOO MUCH FAT AND WILL ELIMINATE THE GREASY TASTE.

Wild Rabbit Casserole

Serves: 4-6
Prep Time: 5 hours

> 2 **rabbits**
> 2 **oz. butter**
> 4 **oz. milk**
> 1 **T. parsley, chopped**
> 1 **T. chives**
> 1 **lg. garlic clove, finely diced**
> 2 **med. carrots, diced**
> 1 **stalk celery, diced**
> 4 **spring onions, chopped**
> 1 **cup bread crumbs**
> 10 **oz. sour cream**
> ½ **tsp. paprika**
> ½ **tsp. pepper**

Soak rabbits in salt water for 3 hours. Bone rabbits. Fry meat in 2 oz. butter for 3-4 minutes. Combine milk, parsley, chives, garlic, carrots, celery and onions in a saucepan and bring to a boil. Cover and simmer for 30 minutes. Pour into a casserole dish, add meat and stir. Sprinkle bread crumbs on top of mixture. Spread sour cream over bread crumbs and sprinkle with paprika and pepper. Cook in 350-degree oven for 1 to 1½ hours. Serve over rice.

Thomas Gluzinski
Alliance, Ohio

SEASON BEFORE FREEZING—SEASON FOODS LIGHTLY BEFORE FREEZING, THEN ADD MORE WHEN REHEATING. CLOVES, PEPPER, GARLIC AND CELERY BECOME STRONGER ON FREEZING; ONION, SALT AND CHILI POWDER WEAKEN.

E-Z Rabbit

Serves: 5-6
Prep Time: 3 hours

> **3-4 rabbits, cut into pieces**
> **salt and pepper**
> **flour**
> **5 lg. potatoes, peeled and cut in chunks**
> **1 lb. carrots, cut in large chunks**
> **2 med. onions, cut in chunks**
> **1 envelope onion soup mix**
> **1 can cream of onion soup**
> **½ cup white wine**
> **water**

Salt and pepper rabbit pieces. Dredge in flour and fry in hot oil until browned. Arrange pieces in large baking pan. Scatter potato and carrot chunks around rabbit. Cover with onion chunks. Mix dry onion soup mix with canned soup in 3 cup measure. Add wine and enough water to measure 3 cups. Pour over rabbit. Cover with foil and bake at 350 degrees for 2 hours. Remove foil last ½ hour of baking.

Matt Markland
Englewood, Florida

UNDERCOOK STARCHY INGREDIENTS FOR FREEZING—
BEANS, RICE AND NOODLES CAN BECOME MUSHY WHEN FROZEN.
POTATOES BECOME ESPECIALLY SOFT.

Grandma's Slow Cooking Hasenpfeffer

Serves: 4-6
Prep Time: 8-10 hours

- 2 **rabbits, cut up**
- 2 **onions, sliced**
- 2 **T. salt**
- 1 **pint cider vinegar**
- 1 **cup boiling water**
- ½ **cup sugar**
- 12 **gingersnaps, crumpled**
- 2 **bay leaves**
- 6 **whole cloves**
- 1 **T. mixed pickling spice**
- 3 **T. flour**
- ½ **cup cold water**

Combine bay leaves, cloves and pickling spice on a three-inch square piece of cheesecloth and tie into bundle. Place rabbit pieces and all ingredients except flour and water in slow cooker in the order given. Cover and cook on low setting for 8 to 10 hours. One hour before serving, turn to high setting. Mix flour into cold water and add to the pot 30 minutes before serving. Remove spice bag before serving.

Leroy Hegge
Erlanger, Kentucky

FREEZING CASSEROLES—FREEZE MOST CASSEROLES BEFORE BAKING, ESPECIALLY WHEN ALL THE INGREDIENTS ARE ALREADY COOKED. EXCEPTIONS TO THIS ARE DISHES THAT CONTAIN UNCOOKED RICE, RAW VEGETABLES OR UNCOOKED MEAT THAT HAS BEEN FROZEN AND THAWED.

Rabbit Stew Bake

Serves: 4-6
Prep Time: 2½-3 hours

BEST SERVED OVER HOT BISCUITS!

   2 **rabbits, cut in serving pieces**
   8 **slices of bacon, cut up**
   ½ **cup flour**
     salt and pepper
   2 **onions, chopped**
   1 **carrot, chopped fine**
   1 **cup water**

Roll rabbit in flour seasoned with salt and pepper. Fry bacon and set aside. Brown rabbit in bacon grease. Add onion while browning. Put rabbit in roasting pan. Add bacon, onions, carrot and water. As it boils down, add more water. Bake at 350 degrees for 2 hours. If not thick enough, add flour, water.

Rick Cooper
Columbus, Indiana

Kentucky Fried Rabbit

Serves: 6
Prep Time: 1½ hours

   2 **lg. rabbits, cut up**
   ½ **cup celery, chopped**
   ½ **tsp. Mrs. Dash (original)**
   1 **bag Shake and Bake (chicken flavor)**
   ½ **lb. butter**

Add rabbit, celery and Mrs. Dash to boiling water. Boil ½ hour. Drain. Use a large plastic bag for Shake and Bake. Put rabbit in bag and shake until pieces of meat are covered. Fry rabbit with butter until crispy brown.

David Worrell
Vincentown, New Jersey

Varying Hare Pot Pie

Serves: 6
Prep Time: 45 minutes

> **2 rabbits, cut up**
> **6 med. potatoes**
> **6 med. carrots**
> **2 med. onions**
> **seasoning**
> **Bisquick**
> **1 cup milk**

PARBOILING TAKES ABOUT 30 MINUTES!

Cut up rabbits into pieces using backs, front and hind legs.
Parboil until done. Remove meat from bones and cut into small
pieces. While meat is cooking, cut up potatoes, carrots and
onions into small pieces and cook in a separate pot until done.
Add all ingredients together in a casserole dish, season to
taste. Make a dough of Bisquick and milk and put on top of
ingredients. Bake at 350 degrees for about 15 minutes, or until
done.

Verne Turner
Fort Plain, New York

A SIMPLE LEFTOVER MEAL—WHEN WARMING UP LEFTOVERS, WRAP THE POTATOES, VEGETABLES AND MEAT SEPARATELY IN ALUMINUM FOIL PACKETS AND PLACE ALL OF THEM IN AN ELECTRIC FRYING PAN FILLED WITH A SMALL AMOUNT OF WATER. THIS WILL STEAM THE LEFTOVERS HOT, AND YOU WON'T HAVE TO WASH SEVERAL DIFFERENT PANS.

Karen's Small Game Casserole

Serves: 4
Prep Time: 1½-2 hours

1 rabbit, cooked and deboned
2 10-oz. pkg. frozen chopped broccoli
1 cup onion, chopped
1 cup celery, chopped
1 stick margarine
1 8-oz. jar Cheez Whiz
1 can cream of mushroom soup
2 cups Minute Rice, cooked

LEFTOVER RABBIT WORKS WELL!

Bake or parboil rabbit until tender and meat falls off bone easily. Cook broccoli according to package, drain thoroughly in colander. Saute onion and celery in margarine until tender. Blend Cheez Whiz and soup into onions and celery. Mix together rabbit, rice, broccoli and cheese mixture. Place in large casserole and bake for 1 hour at 350 degrees.

Terry Quayle
Ishpeming, Michigan

STEAM YOUR ROLLS—TO WARM UP ROLLS FOR A MEAL WITHOUT USING THE OVEN: PLACE A STRAINER ON YOUR KETTLE OF BOILING POTATOES OR VEGETABLES, PUT THE ROLLS IN, COVER WITH FOIL, AND YOU'LL HAVE WARM ROLLS WHEN THE REST OF THE DINNER IS DONE.

Rabbit Supreme No. 1

Serves: 4-6
Prep Time: 25½ hours

> 2 **rabbits, cut up**
> 5 **T. oil**
> **salt and pepper**
> **rosemary**
> ½ **cup brandy**
> 1½ **cups water**
> 18 **sm. onions, peeled**
> 8 **strips bacon, chopped into ¼-inch pieces**
> 1½ **cups Chablis**
> ½ **stick butter**
> 1 **bay leaf**
> ¼ **tsp. herbs**
> 1 **T. parsley**
> **pinch of thyme**

BE SURE CASSEROLE IS LARGE ENOUGH TO HOLD RABBIT!

Coat rabbit with 3 tablespoons oil, then sprinkle with salt, pepper and rosemary. Place in a large glass or porcelain bowl. Add the brandy, cover and refrigerate for 24 hours. The following day, boil the onions for 3 or 4 minutes in 1½ cups of water, then remove. Add the remaining 2 tablespoons oil to a skillet and saute the bacon until crisp. Transfer the bacon to a medium casserole. Leave oil in the skillet. Remove the rabbit pieces from the marinade and use paper towels to dry. Reserve the marinade. Saute the rabbit in the skillet until browned. Do not overcrowd meat or it won't brown. Transfer the rabbit to the casserole with the bacon. Discard the fat from the skillet and deglaze with the Chablis over medium high heat. Then add to the casserole the onions, half the butter, the bay leaf, herbs, parsley and thyme. Cover and bake at 325 degrees until tender, about 45 to 60 minutes. Transfer to a warm serving platter and arrange the onions around the rabbit. Bring drippings in casserole to a boil, put in the remaining butter, stir, cook until reduced to about 1 cup. Spoon over rabbit and serve with small potatoes, parsley and sauteed mushrooms sprinkled with finely chopped garlic.

Gene Leone
Walnut Creek, California

Al's Wild Meat Chili

Serves: 6-8
Prep Time: 1 hour

½ **lb. rabbit**
½ **lb. squirrel**
1½ **T. flour**
1 **T. pure chili powder**
1½ **tsp. salt**
1 **T. onion powder**
½ **tsp. black pepper**
½ **tsp. garlic powder**
1 **cup water**

VENISON IS ALSO GOOD!

Grind rabbit and squirrel meat. Cook until tender and brown. Add remaining ingredients, mix well. Add water slowly while stirring. Cover and simmer over low heat for 30 minutes.

Col. A. E. Preston
Tocco, Georgia

Squirrel Hash

Serves: 3-4
Prep Time: 1 hour

2 **cups squirrel, cooked and diced**
2 **cups sm. potatoes, cubed**
½ **cup chicken broth**
2 **T. onion, minced**
salt and pepper to taste
dash of paprika
¼ **stick of butter**

Mix squirrel, potatoes, broth and onion. Season with salt and pepper. Dust with paprika. Cook in skillet with the melted butter for about 30 minutes over low heat, stirring often.

Rick Cooper
Columbus, Indiana

Barbecued Squirrel

Serves: 4-6
Prep Time: 1 hour

> **3 squirrels, cut up**
> **1 tsp. barbecue spices**
> **1 cup melted butter**
> **1 tsp. Tabasco sauce (optional)**
> **1 tsp. paprika**
> **salt and pepper to taste**
> **1 tsp. rosemary**

Combine melted butter with other ingredients. Charcoal broil the squirrels as you would chicken over coals, basting with butter and spices.

Tom Squier
Aberdeen, North Carolina

Squirrel With Parsley

Serves: 2
Prep Time: 1 hour

DANDELION GREENS PREFERRED!

> **3 squirrels**
> **2 sm. onions, minced**
> **1 cup cold mashed potatoes**
> **4 T. parsley, chopped**
> **salt and pepper**
> **4 T. dandelion greens or watercress, chopped**
> **2 T. butter**

Cook squirrels in salted water for 30 to 45 minutes. Remove meat from bones. Blend together meat, onions, potatoes and parsley. Season to taste with salt and pepper. Form into balls and roll in dandelion greens or water cress. Fry in hot butter.

John Lee
Osceola, Wisconsin

Squirrel Gumbo

Serves: 6-8
Prep Time: 2 hours

> **3 sm. squirrels, cut into serving pieces**
> **¼ cup flour**
> **¼ cup oil**
> **1½ quarts cold water**
> **½ med. onion, chopped**
> **1 bay leaf**
> **1 tsp. whole black peppercorns**
> **salt and pepper to taste**
> **½ lb. smoked sausage, cut into small pieces**
> **¼ cup green onion tops, chopped**
> **¼ cup parsley, chopped**

First, make a brown sauce from the flour and oil by heating oil and then adding flour *slowly* to oil. Stir constantly until sauce is dark brown. Add cold water. When water simmers, stir and add squirrels, onion and seasonings and cook on medium heat for 30 minutes. Add sausage and continue to cook for 1 hour. Add green onion and parsley, stir and serve.

Chris Yezzi
Greenbelt, Maryland

HOT DOG HEAVEN—ROAST WIENERS ON A HAY FORK. HOLD THE TINES OVER THE FIRE FOR A SHORT TIME UNTIL THE FORK IS CLEAN. THEN PUT ON WIENERS. YOU CAN ROAST A LOT AT ONE TIME, THE LONG HANDLE PROTECTS YOU FROM GETTING TOO CLOSE TO THE FIRE, AND IT'S EASY TO TURN AROUND FOR COOKING BOTH SIDES.

The Hunter's Spice Shelf

A special chapter on the use of spices in wild game meals. A dash of spice can be the quickest, least expensive way to bring flavor to those standard recipes. This chapter shows you how, with sections like "Tips On Using Spices" (page 168), "Spices That Save Time And Labor" (page 170) and a special, seven-page "Guide To Spices" from The National Restaurant Association. Plus you'll find a dozen recipes from the Foran Spice Company.

The Hunter's Spice Shelf

More than 300 years ago the word "restaurant" evolved from the popularity of a recipe for spiced broth. That recipe was called a "restorative," and the importance of spices in good cooking has never diminished.

Today, this subject is more important than ever before. Using spices in your wild game recipes is not only a means to better tasting food, but it is also a way to create different dishes that will help you make better use of your harvested game.

A dash of spice can be the quickest, least expensive way to bring individuality to those standard recipes. And today's spice shelf holds many products that will save labor and time in food preparation.

Tips On Using Spices

In most cases spices and herbs should be used to aid and enhance the natural flavor of foods, not overpower them. The overall impression should be one of savoriness without any particular spice dominating. Exceptions to this would be foods such as curry or chili or gingerbread where the character of the dish depends on its spice.

How Much To Add

Since the pungency of each spice differs and its effect on different foods varies, it is not possible to offer a blanket rule for the amount to use. Following recipes that have been well tested is the surest practice. Where no recipe is available, start with about ¼ teaspoon of spice to each pound of meat or pint of sauce or soup. Make this ⅛ teaspoon in the case of red pepper or cayenne and garlic powder. You will probably find that these starter quantities should be increased in many instances, but it is easier to add a spice than it is to subtract one.

When To Add

Ground spices are ready to give up their flavors quickly. When used in a medium to long cooking dish, they should not be added until near the end of the cooking period. In uncooked dishes, such as salad dressings and fruit juices, the spiced liquid should be left standing for several hours to develop good flavor. If it is not possible to let it stand, the liquid should be brought to a boil and cooked, thus letting the heat bring out the flavor.

Whole spices are especially useful in long cooking dishes. They should be added at the beginning of cooking. It is a good idea to place them in a small cheesecloth or muslin bag so that they may be easily removed when the desired flavor level is obtained. This also avoids any chance of pieces of whole spice remaining in the finished dish. Seeds such as poppy and sesame should be toasted before they are used. Whole, or leaf herbs should be crumbled finely just before they are used to release the best flavor.

How To Store Spices

For best results, spices should be stored in as cool and dry a place as possible. Heat robs their flavors and dampness will cake them. Be sure that your spice containers are tightly closed after every use so that their valuable volatile oils are not lost. In very hot climates, it may be practical to place capsicum spices, like paprika and red pepper, in the refrigerator to guard against infestation.

How Long Will They Keep?

If stored properly, spices will retain aroma and flavor for a long period. The whole spices will keep longer than ground spices. The herbs tend to lose flavor a little faster than such items as pepper, ginger, cinnamon, cloves, etc. As a result, many wild game cooks prefer to buy herbs in the whole or leaf form because they will store better.

Spices That Save Time And Labor

Among the newer developments in the spice industry are dehydrated vegetable seasonings like onion, garlic, sweet peppers, celery, mint, parsley and mixed vegetables. These seasoning flakes are labor savers when a recipe calls for one of these vegetables.

If the recipe includes much liquid (as with a stew or sauce) and the flakes are to remain in the liquid for several minutes before the dish is served, it may not be necessary even to rehydrate them. In the case of instant minced onion and parsley flakes, they will rehydrate sufficiently in about five minutes. For sweet pepper flakes, celery flakes and mixed vegetable flakes, you should allow about 20 minutes for rehydration, either before or during cooking.

If, in the case of a salad or garnish, rehydration is indicated, use equal parts of flakes and water for onion and parsley. For celery and sweet pepper, use twice the amount of water as flakes and when rehydrated, strain off the excess water.

One part of instant minced onion or parsley flakes is equal to about four parts of raw product in seasoning strength. One part of celery or sweet pepper flakes is equivalent to about two parts of the raw vegetable.

A Guide To Spices

Allspice: This pea-sized fruit grows in small clusters on a tree. Picked green, this spice shrivels to brown berries after curing. As its name implies, allspice is reminiscent of cinnamon, nutmeg and cloves. Allspice is best used whole when pickling meats and making gravies. Ground, it is best used in baking, relishes and puddings.

Anise: This is a dried greenish-brown seed of a foot-high annual shrub. It is often used in flavoring licorice. Anise is best used in cookies, candies, sweet pickles and as a beverage flavoring. For anise cookies, just add ¼ teaspoon ground anise to cookie batter.

Apple Pie Spice: This is a ground blend of the sweet baking spices, with a predominance of cinnamon. Cloves, nutmeg or mace, allspice and ginger are typical inclusions in Apple Pie

The Hunter's Spice Shelf

Spice. It is good for all fruit pies and pastries.

Basil: Also known as "sweet basil," basil is the cleaned and dried leaves and tender stems of the plant. Belonging to the mint family, it has an aromatic flavor with a pleasing leafy note. Basil is an important seasoning in tomato paste and tomato dishes. It is a standard ingredient in turtle soup and is best used if sprinkled over chops before cooking.

Barbecue Spice: This is a ground blend of many spices such as chili peppers, cumin, garlic, cloves, paprika, salt and sugar. Designed to be the basic seasoning for a barbecue sauce, this spice is also good in salad dressing, meat casseroles, hash brown potatoes, eggs and cheese dishes.

Bay Leaves: Bay leaves are the dried leaves of an evergreen tree. These smooth oblong leaves are deep green on the upper surface and paler beneath. Their flavor is sweet and herbaceous with a delicate floral spice. Bay leaves are best used with stews, spice sauces, pickling and soups. They are excellent for chowder, and good with a variety of meats, such as fricassee of kidney, heart or oxtail.

Caraway Seed: The biennial plant that produces these seeds grows two or three feet high. The seeds are somewhat curved, tapering toward both ends. Their flavoring is a combination of dill and anise with a slight fruitiness. Caraway is widely used in baking, especially rye bread. It is also good sprinkled on pork, liver or kidneys before heating.

Cardamom Seed: This is a tiny brown seed which grows enclosed in a white or green pod. It produces a sweet and spicy taste. Used in the pod, cardamom seed is best used in mixing pickling spice. When the seed is ground, it flavors Danish pastry, bun breads and coffee cakes and improves grape jelly.

Cayenne Pepper: (See "Red Pepper")

Celery Seed: This seed is a minute, olive-brown seed obtained from the celery plant. Celery salt is made by combining celery seed with salt. It has a parsley-nutmeg flavor. Celery seed is excellent in pickling, salads, fish, salad dressings and vegetables. It is also favored in tomato juice cocktails.

Celery Flakes: These are dehydrated, flaked leaves and stalks of vegetable celery. Its use originated in the United States. It is best in soups, stews, sauces and stuffings.

Chili Powder: This is a ground blend of chili peppers, oregano, cumin seed, garlic, salt and sometimes cloves, red pepper and allspice. It is the basic seasoning for Mexican-style cooking, including chili con carne. It is excellent in stew. Also very good in hamburgers.

Cinnamon: This spice comes from the bark of an aromatic evergreen tree. Cinnamon sticks are often used when pickling, preserving and stewing fruits. Ground cinnamon is used in baked goods, often in combination with allspice, nutmeg and cloves. It is the principle mincemeat spice.

Cinnamon Sugar: There are few if any times in cooking and baking when cinnamon isn't accompanied by sugar, and this skillful blend of the two is a very convenient product. It is favored for cinnamon toast and as a quick topping for many other sweet goods.

Cloves: This spice is the dried flower buds of a tree belonging to the evergreen family and are dark brown and dusky red in color. The flavor is characterized by a sweet, pungent spiciness. Whole, cloves work best with roasts, ham and pork. Ground, it is often used with stews. For a tastier meat stew add a small onion studded with 2 or 3 whole cloves.

Coriander: This spice has a sweet, dry, musty character tending toward lavender. It is the dried fruit of a small plant. Whole, coriander is best in poultry stuffings, biscuits and mixed pickles. Ground, it is favored for sausage making. It can also be rubbed on meat before roasting.

Cumin: Cumin is a small dried fruit, oblong in shape, and resembles caraway seeds. The flavor is penetrating. Cumin is an important ingredient in curry and chili powder. It is frequently used in soups.

Curry Powder: A ground blend of as many as 16 to 20 spices, curry powder is designed to give the flavor of Indian curry cookery. Typical ingredients include ginger, cloves, cinnamon, cumin seed, black pepper and red pepper. Curry powder is favored in meat and sauce recipes.

The Hunter's Spice Shelf

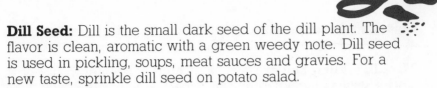

Dill Seed: Dill is the small dark seed of the dill plant. The flavor is clean, aromatic with a green weedy note. Dill seed is used in pickling, soups, meat sauces and gravies. For a new taste, sprinkle dill seed on potato salad.

Fennel: This small seed-like fruit has an agreeable odor and an aromatic, sweet taste somewhat like Anise. It is popular in pickles and Italian sausage. Add a dash to apple pie for an unusually good flavor.

Garlic: Most of the garlic used in dehydrated products is grown in the U.S. This is the most strongly flavored in the allium family and is used in a wide range of dishes. This spice is a very convenient way of adding garlic flavor.

Ginger: This spice comes from the root of a tuberous plant. Its flavor is warm and fragrant, with a pungent spiciness. Whole, it is used in stew and conserves. Ground, it is favored in pot roasts and meats. It is also rubbed on poultry with a mixture of ginger and butter before roasting.

Herb Seasoning: This is a savory blend of herbs, particularly suited to salads and salad dressings. "Herb" specifically refers to the milder flavored leafy products like marjoram, oregano, basil, chervil.

Italian Seasoning: Italian dishes have become so popular in North America that cooks asked for a simple way to achieve the characteristic flavoring of this cuisine. While no one blend could accomplish this completely, it is well known that such seasonings as oregano, basil, red pepper and rosemary are typical of many Italian creations—particularly the popular pastas and pizza.

Mace: This spice is the fleshy growth between the nutmeg shell and the outer husk. Its flavor resembles nutmeg. Whole, mace is excellent in pickling and preserving. Ground, it is essential in cakes and valuable in chocolate dishes.

Marjoram: Marjoram is an herb of the mint family. It has a peculiar, sweet-minty herbaceous type flavor. As a leaf, it is excellent with other herbs in stews, soups and sausage. Ground, it can be sprinkled over cooking meat.

Mint Flakes: These are dehydrated, flaked leaves of

spearmint or peppermint. They yield a strong, sweet flavor and are used in soups, stews and sauces.

Mixed Pickling Spice: This is a mixture of several whole spices, usually including mustard seed, bay leaves, black and white peppercorns, dill seed, red peppers, ginger, cinnamon, mace, allspice, coriander seed, etc. It is used for pickling and preserving meats and to season vegetables and sauces. It is also very good in stews and soups.

Mixed Vegetable Flakes: This is a mixture of dehydrated, flaked vegetables, usually composed of celery, green pepper and carrots. It is a convenient means of seasoning soups, stews, sauces and stuffing.

Mustard: Both white and brown mustard seeds are widely cultivated. The white is mild flavored, while the brown is of the pungent variety from which mustard typically served in Chinese restaurants is made. Whole, the mustard seed is used to garnish pickled meats and hamburgers. Powdered, it is used in meats, sauces and gravies.

Nutmeg: Nutmeg yields a sweet, spicy flavor. It is the kernel of the nutmeg fruit, which grows on a bushy tree that reaches a height of about 40 feet. Ground nutmeg is the most popular. It is used in sauces and puddings. It is said to be the best flavoring for doughnuts.

Onions: Dehydrated onions are a convenient labor saver wherever onion flavor is desired. They are used in soups, stews, sauces, steaks, hamburgers, etc.

Oregano: Also known as origanum and Mexican sage, oregano is a good flavoring for any tomato dish. It is a favorite with pizza and Italian specialities.

Paprika: This is a sweet red pepper that is ground after seeds and stems have been removed. Most paprika sold in North America is mild and sweet in flavor, slightly aromatic and prized for its brilliant red color. It is used as a red garnish. It is an important ingredient in many meat recipes, including goulash and chicken paprika.

Parsley Flakes: These flakes are made in the U.S. from dehydrated parsley leaf and stem material. It is common as a seasoning with soups, meat and sauces. For spiced potato

cakes—made from leftover mashed potatoes—try adding some parsley flakes, onion salt and paprika.

Pepper Black, White: Whole pepper is known as peppercorn. Pepper is a small dried berry from a vine. It is the world's most popular spice. Pepper is warm, pungent and aromatic and adds a spicy tang to almost all foods. Peppercorn is used in pickling, soups and meats. Ground pepper is used in meats, sauces, gravies, soups, etc.

Poppy: This spice comes from the tiny seeds of the poppy plant—about 900,000 poppy seeds equal one pound! It has a crunchy, nut-like flavor, and the best often comes from Holland. It is excellent as a topping for breads, rolls and cookies. It is also good in salads and noodles.

Poultry Seasoning: This is a ground blend of sage, thyme, marjoram and savory. It is best with poultry, veal, pork and fish. For meat loaf, combine it with paprika.

Pumpkin Pie Spice: This is a ground blend of cinnamon, cloves and ginger. It is designed particularly for pumpkin pie, but is also good in gingerbread and breakfast buns.

Red Pepper: This spice is also sold as cayenne, and is often very pungent. There are no heat standards for cayenne or red pepper, so talk with a friend or grocer about the strength of different name brands. It can be used whole in pickles, relishes and hot sauces. Crushed, it is used in highly spiced meats and Italian specialty dishes, including sausages. Ground it is used in meats, sauces and fish.

Rosemary: A spicy herb, rosemary looks like curved pine needles and is sweet and fresh tasting. It is common in soups, stews and roasts.

Seasoned Salt: This all-purpose seasoning goes by different names, including flavor salt. It is a mixture of spices, herbs and salt and can often be found in restaurants on the table next to the salt and pepper. Seasoned salt is especially suited to meats, vegetables and sauces.

Saffron: This spice from Spain is the world's most expensive. It takes 224,000 stigma of a crocus-like flower to make one pound of saffron. Its flavor is distinct. Saffron is used in baked goods, rice and chicken.

Sage: The choicest sage comes from Yugoslavia and Greece. A perennial shrub that is about 2 feet tall is the source of this spice. Sage produces a minty taste in the pork, sausage, meat stuffings and poultry in which it is used. It is also a favorite in salad greens.

Savory: Savory is an herb of the mint family that grows in many climates. Its flavor is sweet and herbaceous, resembling thyme. It is combined with other herbs to make an excellent flavoring for meats, meat dressings and poultry.

Seafood Seasoning: This is a ground blend of approximately the same spices that are used in crab boil and shrimp spice with the addition of salt. It is especially good in seafood sauces because the ground seasoning blends into the sauce completely.

Sesame: Sesame is a small, honey-colored seed with gentle, nut-like flavor and a high oil content. It yields a rich toasted-nut flavor when baked on rolls, breads and buns.

Sweet Pepper Flakes: These are dehydrated, flaked sweet green or red peppers, or a mixture of both. Sweet pepper flakes are a convenient way of adding green or red pepper flavor to sauces, salads, vegetables and casseroles when a fine diced pepper is called for.

Tarragon: Tarragon comes from a perennial plant which forms tall stalks about 4 feet high. This spice produces a minty, herbaceous and anise-like flavor. It is used in sauces, salads, poultry, meats and tomato dishes.

Thyme: A low shrub about a foot high yields thyme. This spice is used in stews, soups and poultry stuffings. It is excellent in sauces, fricassees and chipped beef. Thyme and fresh tomatoes go very well together.

Turmeric: Turmeric is a root of the ginger family, and it is an important ingredient of curry powder. It yields a mild ginger-pepper flavor, and is used with mustard in meats, salads and relishes.

North Woods Jerky

Serves: varies
Prep Time: 24 hours

> **2 lbs. venison, cut in ⅛-inch strips**
> **¼ cup soy sauce**
> **¼ tsp. black pepper**
> **1 T. Worcestershire sauce**
> **¼ tsp. garlic powder**
> **½ tsp. onion powder**

Mix seasonings. Add meat. Let stand for 1 hour. Cover and refrigerate overnight. Place meat on oven racks. Do not overlap. Place in the oven, but not within four inches of the heat source. Place foil on a lower rack to catch drippings. Dry at 150 to 175 degrees Fahrenheit for 6 to 10 hours until dry and almost crisp. Keep the oven door open about 1 inch during the first few hours of drying to allow moisture to escape. Cool on absorbent paper. Pat off beads of accumulated fat. Store in an airtight plastic bag or jar.

Ultimate Meat Loaf

Serves: 6
Prep Time: 1½ hours

> **2 lbs. ground venison and pork mix**
> **1 cup Italian seasoned bread crumbs**
> **2 eggs, beaten**
> **1-1½ cups ricotta cheese**
> **½ cup zucchini, grated**
> **½ cup onion, chopped**
> **¼ cup red pepper or red pimento, chopped**
> **1 tsp. parsley flakes**

Combine all ingredients. Mold into a deep dish or loaf pan. Bake for 1 to 1½ hours at 350 degrees.

Sicilian Burgers

Serves: 4-5
Prep Time: 30 minutes

> **1 lb. ground venison**
> **1 egg, beaten**
> **½ cup Italian seasoned bread crumbs**
> **⅔ cup of spaghetti sauce**
> **3 green onions, diced**
> **salt and pepper to taste**

In a medium bowl, mix all ingredients together and form into patties. Broil or pan fry over medium heat, or try it on an outdoor grill. Add a slice of mozzarella cheese or sauteed mushrooms on top of each burger at the last minute of cooking to add a great touch.

Stir-Fry Pheasant With Pasta And Vegetables

Serves: 4
Prep Time: 30 minutes

> **10-12 oz. pheasant breasts, boneless**
> **1 lb. pasta, cooked and drained**
> **2 sticks of butter, melted**
> **½ cup Italian seasoned bread crumbs**
> **chopped vegetables of your choice**

Cut pheasant breasts into strips. Saute pheasant in one stick melted butter until pheasant is lightly browned. Add ¼ cup of the bread crumbs and mix well to coat the pheasant pieces. Add the chopped vegetables, cooked pasta, the remaining stick of melted butter and ¼ cup seasoned bread crumbs. Continue to stir-fry until vegetables are done.

Mexican Fajitas

Serves: varies
Prep Time: 5 hours

**2 lbs. venison, pheasant or any wild game
   meat
2 T. Fajita seasoning
1 med. onion, sliced
1 green pepper, cut in strips (optional)
1 red pepper, cut in strips (optional)
   flour tortillas
   salsa
   guacamole
   sour cream**

Marinate wild game meat in Fajita seasoning for several hours. Stir fry in a hot skillet until meat is no longer pink. Add onion slices and either green or red pepper strips. Serve on flour tortillas with salsa, guacamole and sour cream.

Venison Kabobs

Serves: 4
Prep Time: 2 hours

**1½ lbs. top round or sirloin venison steak
1 T. barbecue seasoning
2 green or red peppers
½ lb. mushrooms**

On skewers, alternate meat, peppers and mushrooms. Sprinkle kabobs with barbecue seasoning. Cover. Refrigerate for 1 hour. Grill over medium-hot coals until meat is cooked to desired doneness. Allow about 15 minutes for rare meat.

Sicilian Style Poultry

Serves: 4
Prep Time: 30 minutes

> 2 **pheasants, boned and cut in pieces**
> 2 **cups flour**
> 1 **egg, beaten**
> 2 **cups Italian seasoned bread crumbs**
> ¼ **cup oil**
> 1 **green pepper, diced**
>   **mozzarella cheese, sliced**
> 1 **can tomato sauce**

Remove skin from pheasant pieces. Dredge in flour, beaten egg, then bread crumbs. Brown in oil.

Serve with sauteed green peppers or top each piece with a slice of mozzarella cheese and tomato sauce.

Venison Chili

Serves: 4-6
Prep Time: 3 hours

> 2 **lbs. ground venison**
> 1 **lg. onion, diced**
> 2 **16-oz. cans of kidney beans**
>   **dash of Tabasco sauce**
> 1 **cup celery, diced**
> 3 **16-oz. cans stewed tomatoes**
>   **dash of sugar**
> 2 **oz. chili powder**

Combine the onion, 16 oz. kidney beans, Tabasco sauce, celery, stewed tomatoes and sugar in a large kettle; stir. Simmer for 1 hour. Brown venison and drain. Add to the sauce and cook at a low heat for 1 hour. Add the remaining kidney beans and chili powder and cook at low heat for 1 hour.

Cajun-Flavored Venison Soup

SERVE WITH ¼ CUP RICE!

Serves: 8
Prep Time: 3 hours

- 3-4 lbs. venison shanks
- 4 cups water
- 1 28-oz. can crushed tomatoes
- 1 cup celery, chopped
- 1 cup onions, chopped
- 1 tsp. garlic, minced
- 1 T. Cajun seasoning
- 2 beef bouillon cubes
- 2 cups cabbage, chopped
- 1 cup green bell peppers, chopped
- ¼ cup lemon juice
- 2 cups cooked rice

Place venison shanks, water, tomatoes, celery, onion, garlic, seasonings and bouillon in large soup pot. Bring to a boil and reduce the heat. Cover and simmer for 2 hours, stirring occasionally. Remove the shanks and cut the meat from bone into small pieces. Return meat with cabbage and green peppers. Continue to simmer until meat and vegetables are tender. Stir in lemon juice.

Zesty Barbecued Pheasant

Serves: several
Prep Time: 2 hours

- 1 pheasant, cut in pieces
  barbecue seasoning
  barbecue sauce

Sprinkle pheasant with seasoning, cover and refrigerate 1 hour. Place bone side down over medium coals. Grill for 25 minutes or until bone side is well browned. Turn pheasant. Grill 20 to 25 minutes. Brush pheasant with barbecue sauce last 10 minutes.

Cajun Meat Loaf

Serves: several
Prep Time: 1 to 1½ hours

> **4 T. butter**
> **¾ cup onions, chopped**
> **½ cup celery, chopped**
> **½ cup green bell peppers, chopped**
> **¼ cup shallots, chopped**
> **2 tsp. garlic, minced**
> **1 T. Tabasco sauce**
> **1 T. Worcestershire sauce**
> **1 T. Cajun seasoning**
> **½ tsp. ground cumin**
> **½ tsp. ground nutmeg**
> **½ tsp. ground bay leaves**
> **½ cup evaporated milk**
> **½ cup catsup**
> **1½ lbs. ground venison**
> **½ lb. ground pork**
> **2 eggs, beaten**
> **1 cup bread crumbs**

Mix onions, celery, bell peppers, shallots, garlic, Tabasco
sauce, Worcestershire sauce and all the seasonings. Add milk
and catsup. Simmer 10 minutes. Combine eggs, venison, pork
and bread crumbs. Add seasoned mixture and form into a loaf.
Bake at 350 degrees for 1 hour.

Basic Grilled Burgers

Serves: 2-3
Prep Time: 30 minutes

> **1 lb. ground venison**
> **½ tsp. barbecue seasoning**

Mix meat and seasonings, form into patties and grill over
medium-hot coals until meat is cooked to desired doneness.

Big Game

Recommended recipes for elk, moose, caribou, bear and wild pigs. Broil, bake, smoke and fry your big game with these recipes from your fellow NAHC members. You'll find more than 30 big game recipes, like "Elk Scallopini" (page 190) and "Old Trapper's Stew" (page 204).

Bear Tenders

Serves: varies
Prep Time: 1½ hours

  1 **lb. bear meat, cubed**   ← *REMOVE ALL FAT FROM CUBED MEAT!*
  2 **T. margarine**
  pepper to taste
  ¼ **cup pineapple juice**
  ¼ **cup smoked barbecue sauce**

Brown bear cubes in margarine. Add pepper to taste. Pour pineapple juice over meat, simmer 20 minutes. Drain. Coat with barbecue sauce. Add water as needed. Simmer in covered pan for 30 to 45 minutes.

B. Lewandowski
Greenlane, Pennsylvania

Bear Pot Roast

Serves: 6-8
Prep Time: 5 hours

SERVE HOT WITH NOODLES, VEGETABLES AND PINEAPPLE SLICES!

  2 **lb. bear roast**
  1 **lg. onion, chopped**
  1 **bay leaf**
  2 **garlic cloves**
  1 **quart water**
  3 **med. carrots, sliced**
  5 **lg. potatoes, peeled and diced**
  salt and pepper to taste

Place all the ingredients except the carrots and potatoes into a large roasting pan and bake at 325 degrees for 4 hours. Add carrots and potatoes and bake 1 hour longer. Make gravy from juice.

Phil Gereau
Withee, Wisconsin

Frank's Bear Stew

Serves: 2-4
Prep Time: 1-2 hours

- **2 lbs. bear meat, cubed**
- **2 T. olive oil**
- **2 T. flour**
- **¼ tsp. black pepper**
- **⅛ tsp. cayenne pepper**
- **1 tsp. salt**
- **10 juniper berries**
- **1½ pints water**
- **8 med. potatoes**
- **1 sm. can mushrooms (optional)**

HEAP HOT COALS ON DUTCH OVEN COVER!

Cook bear meat with olive oil in small Dutch oven. Cook meat until done. Stir in flour, black pepper, cayenne pepper and salt. When all water and oil is absorbed in flour, add juniper berries, water and diced potatoes. Simmer in closed Dutch oven for 30 minutes. Add small can of mushrooms if desired. Serve with sourdough bread and butter.

Frank Whitley
Orick, California

CORE YOUR PEARS FOR CANNING—TO CORE PEARS FOR CANNING: CUT PEAR IN HALF AND SCOOP OUT THE MIDDLE OF EACH HALF WITH THE ONE-HALF TEASPOON MEASURE OF YOUR METAL MEASURING SPOON SET. THIS MAKES A NICE ROUND HOLLOW IN EACH HALF.

Tore's Bear Kabob

Serves: 6-8
Prep Time: overnight plus 1 hour

> **2 lbs. bear meat, cubed**
> **¾ cup Italian salad dressing**
> **2-3 green peppers**
> **2-3 lg. onions** ← *USE ANY VEGETABLES YOU LIKE!*
> **6 skewers**

Marinate meat overnight in Italian salad dressing. On skewers alternate meat, onion and peppers. Grill over hot coals until well done. Sprinkle with preferred spices. Bear can be substituted with deer, elk, boar or moose.

Ronald Torgersen
Windgap, Pennsylvania

Buffalo Goulash

Serves: 4-6
Prep Time: 1-2 hours

> **1 lb. buffalo meat, ground**
> **3 med. potatoes, cubed**
> **3 med. carrots, diced**
> **1 lg. onion, sliced**
> **salt, pepper and garlic powder to taste**
> **1 can kidney beans, undrained**
> **½ cup tomato catsup**

Brown buffalo meat in a skillet. Add vegetables, salt, pepper, garlic powder and undrained kidney beans. A little water may be added if the mixture is dry. Simmer until vegetables are tender. Add tomato catsup about 10 minutes before vegetables are done.

Marian Keister
Mifflinburg, Pennsylvania

Wagon-Mound Buff-Cutlets

GOES GREAT WITH WILD RICE!

Serves: varies
Prep Time: 2½ hours

> 6 **buffalo cutlets, ½-inch thick**
> 1 **cup onions, chopped**
> 1 **cup cooking oil**
> 8 **T. flour**
> 8 **strips bacon**
> ½ **cup parsley, chopped**
> 2 **cans stewed tomatoes**
> 2 **cups beef stock**

Cook cutlets, onions in oil ½ hour. Remove and coat in flour. Brown bacon with onions. Add parsley, cutlets. Simmer 15 minutes. Add tomatoes, beef stock. Simmer 1 hour.

Rick Sinchak
Warren, Ohio

Arctic Burger

Serves: 4-6
Prep Time: 20 minutes

> 1 **lb. ground caribou**
> 1 **lb. ground moose**
> 4 **tsp. mustard**
> 3 **tsp. Worcestershire sauce**
> 1 **tsp. parsley**
> 5 **T. catsup**
> 1 **cup bread crumbs**
> 1 **T. corn meal**
> ½ **cup milk**
> 12 **strips bacon**

Mix all ingredients except bacon. Shape into large patties. Broil patties for 6 minutes on each side with bacon.

Rick Sinchak
Warren, Ohio

Caribou Stew

Serves: 6
Prep Time: 2 hours

   1 **lb. caribou meat**
   2 **onions, chopped**
   2 **T. garlic**
   2 **T. salt**
   1 **pinch parsley**
   1 **pinch oregano**
5-6 **potatoes, peeled and diced**
   2 **cans sweet peas**
   1 **can carrots**
   1 **lb. bow noodles**
   1 **can tomato paste**

Cook meat until well done. Add onions and spices. Cook for 10 minutes. Add potatoes. Cook until almost done. Then add peas and carrots. Cook noodles in separate pot. Drain when soft. Add to stew. Simmer for approximately 10 minutes and then add tomato paste. Heat and serve.

John Lambert
Bath, Pennsylvania

AN INEXPENSIVE DEODORIZER—AN INEXPENSIVE WAY TO DEODORIZE YOUR KITCHEN FROM ODORS IS TO PUT SOME ORANGE PEELS IN THE OVEN AT 350 DEGREES WITH THE DOOR AJAR FOR A SHORT WHILE.

Calabrase

Serves: 2-4
Prep Time: ½ hour

> 1½ **lbs. caribou, elk or moose meat, cubed**
> **ham leg, cubed**
> 2 **green bell peppers**
> 2 **red bell peppers**
> 2 **med. yellow onions**
> ½ **tsp. oregano**
> ½ **tsp. rosemary**
> ½ **cup parsley, chopped**
> ½ **tsp. fennel seeds**

Marinate meat your favorite way. Cut peppers and onions into
½-inch strips. Fry in large pan, adding ½ the amount of spices.
Cook until half done. Salt and pepper to taste. Option: Add hot
pepper to taste. Set aside.

Heat large fry pan and add oil. Spread meat around in pan and
fry on high. Do not stir. Let meat brown, then add other half of
spices. Turn meat and continue browning. Cook until meat is
half done. Combine pepper and onions with meat. Fry and stir
together for 1 minute. Take out of hot pan and place in warm
dish. Option: Add 1 cup cooked tomato marinara sauce, stir in,
cook 2 minutes. Serve with crusty Italian bread.

Tom Varbero
Harrison, New York

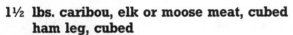

GARLIC FLAVOR ON THE GRILL—A QUICK WAY TO GIVE
BARBECUE FARE A GARLIC FLAVOR IS TO TOSS GARLIC CLOVES ON THE
COALS WHILE THE MEAT GRILLS.

Baked Stuffed Elk Heart

Serves: 2-3
Prep Time: 2-3 hours

1 elk heart
½ lb. beef or pork sausage
herb mix
1 cup milk
2 cups bread crumbs
2 T. margarine

DON'T LET COATING GET TOO BROWN!

Clean heart. Cut open, stuff with sausage and herb mix. Tie closed, place in pot. Cover with water. Boil for 5 minutes; simmer 1 to 2 hours. Remove and wet with milk. Roll in bread crumbs and dot with margarine; repeat to thicken. Roast at 350 to 375 degrees for 30 minutes. Baste with herb butter.

Brian Leavy
Los Alamos, New Mexico

Elk Scallopini

Serves: 6
Prep Time: 1 hour

GREAT OVER RICE OR MASHED POTATOES!

1½ lbs. elk steak, sliced thin
¼ cup olive oil
½ cup onion, chopped fine
3 garlic cloves, chopped fine
½ lb. fresh mushrooms, sliced
flour
1 can tomato sauce
1 cup white wine
1 tsp. Italian seasoning
salt and pepper to taste

Saute onion, garlic in oil. Dredge elk in flour. Add meat and brown. Add all ingredients. Simmer ½ hour.

Ted Marks
San Francisco, California

Elk Mushroom Enchiladas

Serves: 8
Prep Time: 45 minutes

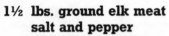

1½ lbs. ground elk meat
      salt and pepper
3 cans cream of mushroom soup
1 4-oz. can mushrooms
1 4-oz. can green chiles, chopped
1 8-oz. carton sour cream
1 cup milk
1 med. onion, chopped
1 pkg. flour tortillas
2 cups grated cheese

Preheat oven to 350 degrees. Fry ground elk until brown, seasoning with salt and pepper. Drain fat. In a large bowl mix remaining ingredients except 1 can mushroom soup, ½ cup milk, cheese and tortillas. Fill tortillas with 2 tablespoons of mixture and roll up, placing in a 9x12x2-inch pan, seam down. Pour the remaining mixture evenly over the top. Bake at 350 degrees for 15 minutes. Remove from oven. Mix remaining can of mushroom soup and milk and pour over enchiladas. Top with grated cheese and return to oven until cheese melts and mushroom topping has heated.

Chris Hugues
Pocatello, Idaho

USE STRAWS FOR SOUP—WHEN SERVING CHILDREN SOUP, GIVE THEM STRAWS TO SUCK UP THE REMAINING BROTH. IT ADDS A BIT OF FUN TO THEIR MEAL AND YOU'LL NEVER AGAIN HAVE TO SCOLD THEM FOR NOT EATING ALL OF THEIR SOUP.

Elk Lasagna

Serves: 4
Prep Time: 1 hour

  10 oz. elk steak, cubed
  8 lasagna noodles
  2 T. butter
     mushrooms, cut up
  1 lg. garlic clove, diced
  1 lg. onion, sliced
  1 tsp. basil leaves
  1 tsp. parsley flakes
  1 16-oz. can whole tomatoes
  1 tsp. salt
  ¼ tsp. pepper
  6 oz. black olives, pitted
  2 T. tomato paste
  8 oz. mozzarella cheese, grated
  ½ cup Parmesan cheese
  16 oz. large curd cottage cheese

ELK OR DEER SAUSAGE GOOD, TOO!

Boil lasagna noodles for 15 minutes. In a fry pan cook elk meat in butter. Add mushrooms, garlic, onion, basil, parsley, tomatoes, salt, pepper and olives. Cook 5 minutes. Add tomato paste. Stir to mix. Put 2 noodles in bottom of casserole dish. Spoon hot mixture on top of noodles. Sprinkle mozzarella and Parmesan cheese on top of mixture, then put cottage cheese on top of cheese and add 2 more noodles. Then repeat the steps again. Two noodles should be left to top off the mixture. Bake at 350 degrees for 30-35 minutes.

Matt Olson
Toutle, Washington

TO PRESERVE CASSEROLES—CHILL HOT CASSEROLES RAPIDLY. SET PAN OF HOT FOOD IN ICE WATER; COOL TO ROOM TEMPERATURE. WRAP, LABEL AND FREEZE.

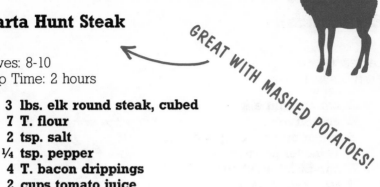

Sparta Hunt Steak

Serves: 8-10
Prep Time: 2 hours

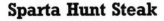
GREAT WITH MASHED POTATOES!

   3 **lbs. elk round steak, cubed**
   7 **T. flour**
   2 **tsp. salt**
 ¼ **tsp. pepper**
   4 **T. bacon drippings**
   2 **cups tomato juice**
   1 **cup carrots, diced**
   1 **cup celery, diced**
   1 **cup onion, chopped**

Dredge meat in seasoned flour. Brown in drippings; remove. Add remaining flour and tomato juice. Stir until thick. Boil 4 minutes. Add meat, other ingredients. Cover and simmer for 50 minutes.

Rick Sinchak
Warren, Ohio

Beth's Elk Salami

Serves: varies
Prep Time: 25 hours

    2 **lbs. ground elk**
    2 **T. Morton's Quick Salt**
  ¼ **tsp. onion powder**
  ⅛ **tsp. garlic powder**
1½ **tsp. liquid smoke**
    1 **cup water**
    2 **T. peppercorns**

Mix all ingredients. Form into 3 sticks. Wrap in plastic wrap or foil and chill in refrigerator for 24 hours. Unwrap and lay on baking sheet. Bake for 1 hour at 350 degrees.

Jay Conner
Topeka, Kansas

Elk Meatballs

Serves: 6
Prep Time: 1 hour

 2 lbs. ground elk
 ¼ cup olive oil
 6 green onions, chopped fine
 ½ T. garlic powder
 ½ cup parsley, chopped fine
 1 tsp. Italian seasoning
 1 cup bread crumbs
 2 eggs
 1 sm. pkg. frozen chopped spinach
 salt and pepper to taste
 2 jars spaghetti sauce with mushrooms
 1 cup water
 1 cup grated cheese, optional

WASH AND DRAIN SPINACH BEFORE USING!

Combine all ingredients except spaghetti sauce, water and cheese. (Note: Drain spinach well.) Form into meatballs, approximately 20. Brown in olive oil. Add spaghetti sauce and water. Simmer with meatballs for 45 minutes. Serve over pre-cooked spaghetti. Add grated cheese to taste.

Ted Marks
San Francisco, California

MEASURING YOUR SHORTENING—FOR EASIER MEASURING OF SHORTENING: USE A 2 CUP MEASURING CUP. FOR ½ CUP OF SHORTENING, FILL THE CUP WITH 1½ CUPS OF WATER AND SPOON SHORTENING INTO THE CUP UNTIL THE WATER LEVEL HITS 2 CUPS. CHANGE THE WATER LEVEL ACCORDING TO YOUR REQUIREMENTS.

Teriyaki Elk Kabobs

Serves: 6
Prep Time: 30 minutes

- 1½ **lbs. elk steak, cubed**
- 2 **green peppers, cubed**
- 15 **cherry tomatoes**
- ½ **lb. fresh mushrooms**
- 1 **med. onion**
  Teriyaki Marinade:
- ½ **cup soy sauce**
- 2 **T. molasses**
- ¼ **cup salad oil**
- 2 **tsp. ground ginger**
- 2 **tsp. dry mustard**
- 6 **garlic cloves, minced**

TRY ZUCCHINI, CUCUMBER, OLIVES, RED PEPPERS, ARTICHOKE FOR VARIETY!

Marinate meat for 15 minutes. Drain. Place ingredients on skewers, alternating meat with fresh vegetables. Grill 5 to 10 minutes, turning frequently and basting with marinade.

Debora Ann Skeim
Kalispell, Montana

Beth's Mushroom Baked Steak

Serves: 4
Prep Time: 9 hours

- 4 **elk steaks**
  Italian dressing
- 1 **can mushroom soup**
- 1 **cup milk**

Marinate steaks in Italian dressing for 6-8 hours. Brown in cast iron skillet. Drain. Mix mushroom soup and milk. Pour over steaks and bake approximately 1 hour at 325 degrees. Serve.

Jay Conner
Topeka, Kansas

Elk Gyro Burgers

Serves: 4
Prep Time: 25 minutes (chill overnight)

> 1 **lb. ground elk**
> 1 **lb. ground lamb**
> 1 **egg**
> ¼ **cup water**
> ½ **cup bread crumbs**
> ¼ **tsp. garlic powder**
> ¼ **tsp. cinnamon**
> ¼ **tsp. allspice**
> ½ **tsp. thyme**
> ½ **tsp. sweet basil**
> 2 **tsp. oregano**
> 1 **T. sugar**
> 1 **cup yogurt (plain)**
> 5 **T. sour cream**
> 1 **T. sugar**
> 2 **T. parsley flakes**
> ¼ **cup onions, diced**
> ¼ **cup cucumber, diced**

TRY A DASH OF CAYENNE PEPPER!

Combine first 12 ingredients. Mix well. Cover, chill overnight. Combine remaining ingredients for sauce. Mix well. Cover, chill overnight. Shape meat into patties 1-inch thick by 4-inches wide. Cook 4 minutes on each side. Serve on Pita bread or homemade buns with lettuce, sliced tomatoes, onions and yogurt sauce on top.

Debora Ann Skeim
Kalispell, Montana

FREEZE YOUR CHIPS—KEEP POTATO CHIPS, CRACKERS AND PRETZELS IN THE FREEZER IN THE SUMMER. THEY'LL ALWAYS BE FRESH AND CRISP.

Boar-Head Beans

Serves: 8-10
Prep Time: overnight plus 8 hours

> **1 lb. boar meat, cut in strips**
> **2 lbs. navy beans**
> **4 strips bacon**
> **½ cup brown sugar**
> **1 tsp. dry mustard**
> **4½ tsp. salt**
> **½ cup molasses**
> **1 tsp. onion powder**

Soak beans overnight. Drain. Boil 40 minutes. Brown meat with bacon. Mix with beans, other ingredients. Add ½ cup boiling water. Bake at 250 degrees for 6 hours; add water as needed. Remove lid last hour.

Rick Sinchak
Warren, Ohio

Wild Boar Nabe

Serves: 4-6
Prep Time: 2 hours

> **1 lb. wild boar meat, cubed**
> **1 cup fresh or dried mushrooms**
> **1 cup carrots, sliced**
> **2 cups potatoes, diced**
> **½ cup cooking Sake or other cooking wine**
> **2 T. soy sauce**
> **2 T. vinegar**
> **¼ cup miso paste**

Cover meat with water and boil. After partially cooked, add other ingredients. Serve when vegetables are soft.

Norman Lund
Kofu Shi, Japan

Breaded Wild Boar Chops

Serves: 4
Prep Time: 45 minutes

4-6 boar chops, ½- to ¾-inch thick
1½ tsp. garlic salt
3 tsp. flour
¼ cup fine bread crumbs
1 tsp. onion powder
¼ cup milk

DON'T OVERCOOK VEGETABLES! SERVE WITH CHINESE NOODLES!

Mix salt, flour, bread crumbs, onion powder and milk. Coat both sides of chops and place on baking pan. Bake at 350 degrees for about 45 minutes or until baked.

Joe Albanese
North Jackson, Ohio

"Won't Boar You!"

Serves: 6-8
Prep Time: overnight plus 1 hour

2 cups wild boar, cubed
¼ cup soy sauce
½ cup vinegar
salt and pepper to taste
1 T. garlic salt
¼ cup flour
½ cup oil
1½ cups broccoli spears
2 lg. onions, sliced
2 cups cooked rice

ADD MISO PASTE IF TOO SWEET!

Marinate meat overnight in vinegar and soy sauce. Drain and lightly flour. Brown in oil. Add vegetables, cook lightly. Add meat and rice. Stir. Cook 5 minutes.

Ronald Torgersen
Windgap, Pennsylvania

Doug's Wild Hog Stew

Serves: 8
Prep Time: 2½ hours

    4 lbs. wild boar, cut in large chunks
    ½ lb. Anaheim sweet peppers
    1 lb. bell peppers
    1 lb. mushrooms
    1 lb. tomatillos
    1 T. olive oil
    8 oz. tomato sauce
    6 oz. tomato paste
    48 oz. stewed tomatoes, drained
    6 T. corn flour
    1 tsp. cayenne pepper
    1½ tsp. salt
    ¼ cup chili powder
    1 T. cumin
    1 T. paprika
    1 tsp. oregano
    1 tsp. onion powder
    1 tsp. garlic powder
    1 T. fruit brandy
    ¼ cup lemon juice
    2 tsp. Worcestershire sauce

In a large skillet saute peppers, mushrooms and tomatillos in olive oil until tender. Add meat and stir until brown. Add remaining ingredients. Mix thoroughly. Cook on low heat for 2 hours, stirring frequently.

Douglas Cuciz
San Jose, California

MORE PUCKER—HEAT LEMONS BEFORE SQUEEZIN' THEM. YOU'LL GET TWICE AS MUCH JUICE PER LEMON.

Doug's Wild Hog Chili

TASTES BETTER REHEATED!

Serves: 5
Prep Time: 2 hours

     2 lbs. wild boar, cut in chunks
     8 oz. tomato sauce
     6 oz. tomato paste
    24 oz. water
     5 T. corn flour
     1 tsp. red cayenne pepper
  1½ tsp. salt
    ¼ cup chili powder
     1 T. cumin
     1 T. paprika
     1 tsp. oregano
     1 tsp. onion powder
     1 tsp. garlic powder
    24 oz. pinto beans

Brown meat in a large skillet. Add tomato sauce and paste to
meat, simmer. In a different pot combine water, corn flour,
pepper, salt, chili powder, cumin, paprika, oregano, onion
powder and garlic powder. Add mixture to browned meat and
tomato sauce. Stir and cook ½ hour on low heat to blend
flavors. Add pre-cooked pinto beans and mix thoroughly. Cook
on low heat for 1½ hours.

Douglas Cuciz
San Jose, California

ADD CHILI POWDER NEAR END—CHILI POWDER SHOULD BE
ADDED TOWARDS THE END OF THE COOKING PERIOD BECAUSE IT IS
READILY DESTROYED AND DILUTED BY HEAT.

Santa Catalina Boar

Serves: 4
Prep Time: 2-3 hours

 2 lbs. boar meat, cubed
¼ cup flour
 1 tsp. salt
   pepper to taste
 3 T. bacon fat
 1 med. onion, chopped
 1 garlic clove, diced
 4 cups water
½ tsp. rosemary
 1 T. parsley flakes
 4 potatoes, peeled
 4 carrots, peeled
 4 sm. onions, peeled and sliced

DEPENDING ON AGE OF BOAR, THIS SHOULD TAKE 1-2 HOURS!

Coat boar in flour mixed with salt and pepper. Heat bacon fat in a deep pan and brown meat on all sides. Add chopped onion and garlic clove and cook 5 minutes longer. Add water and seasoning and cook covered until meat is tender. Add potatoes, carrots and small onions and cook another 30 minutes or until vegetables are done.

Alan Conzelmann
Arcadia, California

A SMART KNIFE PROTECTOR—KEEP YOUR KNIVES SHARP AND PREVENT CUTS WHEN SEARCHING FOR THINGS IN A DRAWER. CUT A PIECE OF CARDBOARD THREE TIMES AS WIDE AS A KNIFE BLADE AND AS LONG AS THE BLADE. FOLD THE CARDBOARD IN HALF. STAPLE THE SIDES AND ONE END. INSERT THE KNIFE BLADE INTO THE CARDBOARD AND STORE IN DRAWER.

Old Vienna Moose & Noodles

Serves: 10-15
Prep Time: 2 hours

BEST SERVED WITH LARGE EGG NOODLES!

    5 lbs. moose meat, cubed
    flour
    1 cup butter
    paprika
    6 cups onions, chopped
    2 green peppers, sliced
    4 cups beef broth
    2 bay leaves

Dredge moose in seasoned flour. Brown in butter. Add other ingredients, cover. Simmer for 1 hour.

Rick Sinchak
Warren, Ohio

Moose Cordon Bleu

Serves: 4
Prep Time: 45 minutes

    4 moose loins, cut 1½-inch thick
    ½ lb. shaved ham, sliced thin
    4 slices Swiss cheese
    2 eggs
    ¼ cup milk
    Italian seasoned bread crumbs
    2 T. oil
    garlic powder
    1 lemon
    fresh parsley

FLAVOR OIL WITH PINCH OF GARLIC POWDER!

Butterfly loins. Insert ham, cheese. Fold and secure with toothpick. Mix eggs, milk. Dip loins in mixture, coat with crumbs. Brown in oil. Top with lemon slices, parsley.

Steve Lake
Florissant, Missouri

Moose Ball Soup

Serves: 6-8
Prep Time: 1½ hours

   1 lb. ground moose
   6 quarts soup stock
   2 eggs
   ½ cup bread crumbs
   ½ cup onion, chopped
   ½ tsp. garlic powder
   2 T. parsley, chopped
   1 cup instant rice

Simmer stock 20 minutes. Mix moose, eggs, bread crumbs, onions and garlic powder. Form into balls. Add with parsley to kettle. Simmer 35 minutes. Add rice, simmer 15 minutes.

Rick Sinchak
Warren, Ohio

V-8 Moose

SERVE PLAIN OR WITH RICE!

Serves: 3-4
Prep Time: 1 hour

   2 lbs. moose steak, cubed
   1 cup flour
   salt and pepper
   1 lg. onion, sliced
   1 cup mushrooms
   1 tsp. black pepper
   ⅛ tsp. garlic powder
   ⅛ tsp. dill weed
   2 cups V-8 juice

Dredge moose in seasoned flour. Brown, add onion, mushrooms, spices. Cover and simmer until onions are soft, about 10 minutes. Add V-8 juice. Simmer 20 minutes covered.

Mike Costello
Birch Run, Michigan

Old Trapper's Stew

Serves: 10
Prep Time: 2½ hours

>   2 lbs. moose stew meat
>   1 lb. ground caribou
>   2 tsp. salt
>   ½ cup flour
>   4 strips bacon, chopped
>   3 cups warm water
>   3 T. Worcestershire Sauce
>   1 can stewed tomatoes
>   1 tsp. dry mustard
>   5 potatoes, cut in quarters
>   1 cup celery, chopped
>   1 onion, sliced

Coat meat with salt and flour. Brown with bacon. Add other ingredients. Form into meatballs. Simmer for 2 hours.

Rick Sinchak
Warren, Ohio

Moose Pot Roast

Serves: 8
Prep Time: 4 hours

>   6-7 lb. moose roast
>   6 potatoes, peeled and sliced
>   6 carrots, sliced
>   4 onions
>   1 pkg. onion soup mix
>   1 16-oz. bottle A-1 sauce
>   1 10-oz. can cream of mushroom soup

Place moose roast in roasting pan. Add balance of ingredients and cover with aluminum foil. Roast at 350 degrees for 4 hours.

Rocco Palumbo
Wellington, Maine

Polynesian Moose Bites

Serves: 6
Prep Time: 1 hour

2 lbs. ground moose
⅓ cup quick uncooked oats
1 can water chestnuts, chopped
2 T. soy sauce
1 sm. onion, chopped
½ tsp. garlic salt
1 egg
½ cup milk
¾ cup firmly packed brown sugar
2 T. cornstarch
1 8-oz. can crushed pineapple, drained
    (reserve juice)
1 cup beef bouillon
½ cup vinegar
2 T. soy sauce
⅓ cup green pepper, chopped

Combine first eight ingredients and form into small meatballs.
Brown in shortening and drain well. Mix brown sugar and
cornstarch. Add juice from pineapple, bouillon, vinegar and soy
sauce. Bring to boil, stirring constantly until clear and thick. Boil
for 1 minute. Stir in pineapple and green pepper. Add sauce to
meatballs and simmer 5-10 minutes. Serve hot.

John Fisher
Logansport, Indiana

SOFTEN YOUR BROWN SUGAR—TO SOFTEN BROWN SUGAR
THAT HAS GOTTEN DRY AND HARD, POUR SUGAR INTO A DISH. DAMPEN A
CLOTH WHICH YOU HAVE FOLDED TO SEVERAL THICKNESSES, AND PLACE
THE CLOTH OVER THE DISH AND LET SIT OVERNIGHT. THE NEXT MORNING
THE SUGAR WILL BE NICE AND SOFT.

Spaghetti Moose Casserole

Serves: 2-4
Prep Time: 1 hour

1 lb. ground moose
2½ cups spaghetti sauce
7 oz. spaghetti
2 T. butter
⅓ cup Parmesan cheese
2 eggs
1 cup cottage cheese
2 cups mozzarella cheese

Brown moose. Add sauce. Cook spaghetti, drain and add
butter, well- beaten eggs and Parmesan cheese. Mix well. In
9x13-inch greased pan, add spaghetti, cottage cheese, meat
mixture. Bake uncovered at 350 degrees for 20 to 30 minutes.
Sprinkle with mozzarella cheese. Bake 5 minutes.

John Fisher
Logansport, Indiana

Triumphant Moose Steaks

Serves: 4
Prep Time: 1½ to 2 hours

1½ lb. steak
1 tsp. dry mustard
4 tsp. cornstarch
½ tsp. salt
¼ tsp. pepper
1 cup onion, sliced
1 carrot, diced
1½ cups tomatoes

BEST SERVED OVER
BROWNED POTATOES
AND BAKED APPLES!

Nick edges of steak. Mix dry ingredients. Pound into steak.
Sear and cover with vegetables. Bake covered 1½ hours.

Debi West
Waterloo, Illinois

Misc. Game

Uncommon wild game recipes from NAHC
members. You'll find recipes for groundhogs,
gators and coons in this chapter.

Browning Bag Groundhog

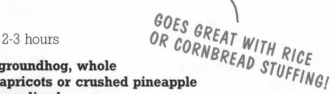

GOES GREAT WITH RICE OR CORNBREAD STUFFING!

Serves: 2-4
Prep Time: 2-3 hours

1 sm. groundhog, whole
1 can apricots or crushed pineapple
6 apples, sliced
salt and pepper to taste

Parboil meat until tender. Drain and fill with apples. Salt and pepper, then coat with apricots or crushed pineapple. Bake at 300 degrees until well browned.

Tom Squier
Aberdeen, North Carolina

Raccoon Roast

Serves: 4
Prep Time: 2 hours

1 raccoon
water
1 tsp. baking soda
salt and pepper
3 cups bread crumbs
2 T. butter, melted
1 sm. onion, chopped
3 stalks celery, chopped
1 egg
½ cup milk

Parboil meat 30 minutes with baking soda. Drain, season with salt and pepper. Combine bread crumbs with remaining ingredients and stuff raccoon. Roast in 375-degree oven for 1½ hours. Drain fat and add water as needed. Before serving, rub with a cloth soaked in vinegar.

Marian Keister
Mifflinburg, Pennsylvania

Chicken Fried Groundhog

Serves: 2-4
Prep Time: 1½ hours

> **2 groundhogs, cut up**
> **1 egg**
> **¾ cup milk**
> **1 cup flour**
> **1 tsp. salt**
> **¼ tsp. pepper**
> **oil**

MAKE SURE TO SOAK GROUNDHOGS IN SALTWATER FIRST!

Parboil meat 20 minutes. Drain and wipe dry. Mix other ingredients. Dip meat in batter and brown in hot oil. Add water to skillet, cover and reduce heat. Simmer until tender.

Tom Squier
Aberdeen, North Carolina

Alligator Stew

Serves: 4-6
Prep Time: 1 hour

> **2 lbs. alligator meat, cut in small pieces**
> **½ cup oil**
> **½ cup green onions, chopped**
> **½ cup bell peppers, chopped**
> **½ cup onions, chopped**
> **½ cup celery, chopped**
> **2 T. ground parsley**
> **1 10-oz. can tomatoes**

RED ONIONS TASTE BEST!

Put ½ cup oil in a pot and brown alligator meat in the oil. Add remaining ingredients, cover the pot and cook over medium heat for about 30 to 40 minutes. Stir occasionally. Serve over cooked rice.

Chris Yezzi
Greenbelt, Maryland

Baked Groundhog In Sour Cream And Mustard

Serves: 2-4
Prep Time: overnight plus 1½ hours

> 1 **med. groundhog, cut up**
> **flour**
> **salt and pepper to taste**
> 5 **T. butter**
> **spiced mustard**
> 4 **slices bacon (smoked)**
> 1 **onion, diced**
> ½ **cup carrots, thinly sliced**
> ½ **cup mushrooms, sliced**
> 3 **T. parsley, chopped**
> 1 **T. rosemary, chopped (optional)**
> 1 **tsp. Kitchen Bouquet**
> 1 **cup sour cream**
> ½ **cup sweet cream**

Soak pieces overnight in salted water, drain and pat dry. Roll in flour, salt and pepper and saute in butter until well browned. Spread spiced mustard on both sides and place bacon strips in a shallow baking dish. Saute the onion, carrots and mushrooms and then add the parsley, rosemary and Kitchen Bouquet. Add salt and pepper to taste. Over low heat, stir in the sour cream and sweet cream. Pour over the meat in the baking dish and bake at 350 degrees for about 45 minutes or until tender. Add a little more cream later on to keep the meat moist.

Tom Squier
Aberdeen, North Carolina

TO FREEZE BREAKFAST WAFFLES—A CONVENIENT PACKAGE FOR FREEZING LEFTOVER BREAKFAST WAFFLES IS A FLAT BUTTER BOX. THREE WAFFLES FIT IN EACH BOX AND CAN EASILY BE WARMED IN THE TOASTER ANOTHER DAY.

Ragout Supremo

Serves: 6
Prep Time: 3½ hours

> 2 **lbs. game meat, cubed**
> 1 **cup beans**
> 3 **cups water**
> 1 **cup seasoned flour**
> 2 **T. oil**
> 1 **cup red wine**
> 1¼ **tsp. salt**
> 1 **bay leaf**
> ½ **tsp. thyme**
> ¼ **tsp. pepper**
> 2 **garlic cloves, pressed**
> 2 **lg. potatoes, cubed**
> 12 **pearl onions**

Combine beans and water and bring to a boil. Turn off heat and let beans sit for an hour. Return to a boil and let simmer for an hour. Meanwhile, coat meat with seasoned flour and brown in a six-quart pan with the oil. Drain beans and add to the meat along with 1 cup of red wine, salt, bay leaf, thyme, pepper and garlic. Stir and let simmer for about 1 hour. Then add potatoes and onions and let cook until the meat is tender and the vegetables are done. Add water as needed while cooking.

Gene Leone
Walnut Creek, California

CREAMIER CEREAL—WHEN COOKING OATMEAL START IT COOKING WITH COLD WATER INSTEAD OF BOILING WATER AS USUALLY IS DIRECTED ON THE BOX. YOU WILL FIND THAT THE TEXTURE OF THE CEREAL IS MUCH SMOOTHER AND CREAMIER.

Helen's Green Chile Game Stew

Serves: 4
Prep Time: overnight plus 1 hour

> **2 cups slivered game meat**
> **1 T. olive oil**
> **2 T. red wine vinegar**
> **2 tsp. Worcestershire sauce**
> **1 T. barbecue sauce**
> **1 med. onion, chopped**
> **2 T. cooking oil**
> **1 tsp. minced garlic**
> **salt, pepper, seasonings to taste**
> **1 15-oz. can pinto beans**
> **1 4-oz. can chopped green chiles, mild or hot.**
> **1 pkg. "au jus" gravy mix**
> **2 cups water**
> **1 T. flour**
> **1 T. margarine**

Combine olive oil, vinegar, Worcestershire sauce and barbecue sauce for marinade. Marinate meat overnight in refrigerator, stirring once. Saute onion in 1 tablespoon. oil until soft and beginning to brown; add garlic and saute 1 minute. Drain meat, reserving marinade, and saute meat with onion until meat loses red color; sprinkle generously with salt, black pepper and other seasonings to taste. Add more oil as necessary to saute meat. Add beans and chiles, cook on medium heat for 5 minutes, stirring occasionally. Dissolve au jus mix in 2 cups water and add to above; add reserved marinade, bring to a boil, reduce heat and simmer for 5 minutes. Mix 1 tablespoon flour with 1 tablespoon margarine; stir into stew and continue to simmer until stew begins to thicken.

Brian Leavy
LosAlamos, New Mexico

SEND US YOUR GAME RECIPE

Title: _____

Serves: _____

Prep Time: _____

Ingredients:

_____
_____
_____
_____
_____
_____
_____
_____

Directions:

_____ fold here
_____
_____
_____
_____
_____
_____
_____
_____
_____
_____
_____
_____
_____
_____
_____
_____

Your NAHC Member # _____

Your Name _____

Address _____

City/State/Zip _____

**North American Hunting Club
P.O. Box 3401
Hopkins, MN 55343**

A Great Gift Idea...
The NAHC Wild Game Cookbook!

Order extra copies of the 1990 Cookbook for your friends and family. They make great gifts —fun to read and practical as well!

You'll also like to have a second copy to keep at the cabin or in with your camping gear.

Send your order in now and get yours at the special Member's price of only $9.95 each. (Non-members pay $14.95)

North American Hunting Club
P.O. Box 3402
Hopkins, MN 55343

(tape or staple here)

Hunters belong in the NAHC ...
and it's so *simple* to join!
Cut out, fold and mail the card below.

- *North American Hunter* magazine
- Keeping Track member news
- Swap Hunts with fellow members
- Hunting Reports on guides/outfitters
- Approved Outfitters & Guide Booklet
- Free Hunts Contest
- New Product & Field Test Reports
- Products & Service Discounts
- Access to Club land
- Your photo in Member Shots
- Big Game Awards, and much, much more!

fold here

ENROLLMENT FORM

Count me in . . .
I want to increase my hunting skills and pleasure.

Here are my $18 annual dues for membership in the North American Hunting Club. I understand my membership will start immediately upon receipt of this application and continue for 12 months.

Name _____
PLEASE PRINT

Address _____

City _____ State _____ Zip _____

Check One:
☐ Check for $18 enclosed
☐ Bill my Master Card/VISA

Credit Card No._____ Exp. Date_____

Signature_____

90 WGCB

If recommended by current member:

Name _____ NAHC No._____

- -

(tape or staple here)

Index

ALLIGATOR
stew, 209

BEAR
kabob, 186
pot roast, 184
stew, 185
tenders, 184

BUFFALO
goulash, 186
wagon-mound cutlets, 187

CARIBOU
arctic burger, 187
calabrase, 189
caribou stew, 188
old trapper's stew, 204

DOVE
boogie, 122
brandon, 121
country style, 123

creamed casserole, 120
special, 109
kabobs, 122

DUCK
a l'orange, 113
barbecued, 139
coot soup, 138
marinated, 136
roast, 115
smoked, a l'orange, 118
wild roast, 137

ELK
baked, stuffed heart, 190
calabrase, 189
gyro burgers, 196
kabobs, teriyaki, 195
lasagna, 192
meatballs, 194
mushroom enchiladas, 191
beth's salami, 193
scallopini, 190
sparta hunt steak, 193
steak, beth's, 195